THE WONDER EFFECT

THE WONDER EFFECT

AN ADVENTUROUS GUIDE FOR IGNITING YOUR PASSIONS AND PURSUING YOUR CALLING

ADAM HASTON

IZZARD INK PUBLISHING
www.izzardink.com

Copyright © 2025 by Adam Haston

All rights reserved. Except as permitted under the U.S. Copyright Act of 1976, no part of this publication may be reproduced, distributed, or transmitted in any form or by any means, or stored in a database or retrieval system, electronically or otherwise, or by use of a technology or retrieval system now known or to be invented, without the prior written permission of the author and publisher.

Library of Congress Cataloging-in-Publication Data

Names: Haston, Adam author
Title: The wonder effect : an adventurous guide for igniting your passions and pursuing your calling / Adam Haston.
Description: First edition. | [Salt Lake City] : Izzard Ink Publishing, [2025]
Identifiers: LCCN 2024060497 (print) | LCCN 2024060498 (ebook) | ISBN 9781642281149 hardback | ISBN 9781642281132 paperback | ISBN 9781642281125 ebook | ISBN 9781642281156 ebook other
Subjects: LCSH: Self-actualization (Psychology) | Self-realization | Wonder Classification: LCC BF637.S4 H369 2025 (print) | LCC BF637.S4 (ebook) DDC 158.1--dc23/eng/20250514
LC record available at https://lccn.loc.gov/2024060497
LC ebook record available at https://lccn.loc.gov/2024060498

Designed by Daniel Lagin
Cover Design by Andrea Ho
Cover Images: Andrea Ho

First Edition

Contact the author at info@izzardink.com

eBook ISBN: 978-1-64228-112-5
Paperback ISBN: 978-1-64228-113-2
Hardback ISBN: 978-1-64228-114-9

Audiobook ISBN: 978-1-64228-115-6

To Esther: Your confidence, trust, and love have given me the strength to explore and experience countless amazing and fun things these last two decades. I can't believe where we have gone and what we have built with our remarkable family of five boys and two girls. I couldn't have asked for a more devoted and supportive life partner.

Mendel, Miriam, Devora Leah, Zalman, Yossi, Chaim Meir, and Shimmy: You are my inspiration for writing this book. I hope it helps you to explore life with more wonder, and I look forward to participating in all of your adventures!

CONTENTS

INTRODUCTION   1

CHAPTER 1: **CRUSH FALSE IDOLS**   17

CHAPTER 2: **KNOW YOURSELF**   49

CHAPTER 3: **LIFE AS A CURRICULUM**   75

CHAPTER 4: **EXPLORE ON YOUR OWN**   99

CHAPTER 5: **BE ADVENTUROUS**   121

CHAPTER 6: **EMBRACE FAILURE**   143

CHAPTER 7: **SET YOUR COMPASS**   167

CHAPTER 8: **SERVE OTHERS**   185

CONCLUSION   201

ACKNOWLEDGMENTS   211

ABOUT THE AUTHOR   217

INTRODUCTION

Have you ever wondered what could be possible for your life? But then, you let doubt and the harsh realities of life pull you back from that beguiling stream of thought?

What if you kept wondering, then let yourself wander a bit? What might happen? And what does it even mean to wonder and wander? Philosophically, the words *wonder* and *wander* share a connection through their exploratory and questioning nature, albeit in slightly different ways. First, they both suggest exploration and curiosity about the world. *Wonder* often refers to a sense of awe, amazement, or curiosity about something; while *wander* typically involves physical movement and exploration of your surroundings.

Second, both words seek meaning and understanding. When you wonder about something, you are often pondering its significance or trying to comprehend its nature. When you wander, you may be searching for answers, insights, or experiences that can broaden your understanding of the world.

Third, *wondering* and *wandering* require being open to new experiences and perspectives, which is essential for growth and learning. Whether you are wondering about the mysteries of the universe or wandering through unfamiliar landscapes, you are embracing the unknown and being receptive to whatever insights or discoveries may come your way. Both concepts involve a degree of contemplation, introspection, and reflection. While the two words may seem different on the surface, they both encompass a philosophical view toward the world and its mysteries.

Dante Alighieri's *Inferno*, translated by Henry Wadsworth Longfellow, details an experience many of us have at some point where we suddenly "wake up" from a wandering slumber, like living life on autopilot, so to speak, not really paying attention to things until we realize we are lost. Not lost in the physical sense, but lost in a deeply existential way. Lost because we've abandoned ourselves. Lost because all sense of wonder has been snuffed out by busyness, overwhelm, and stress.

> Midway upon the journey of our life
> I found myself within a forest dark,
> For the straightforward pathway had been lost.
> I cannot well repeat how there I entered,

INTRODUCTION

> So full was I of slumber at the moment
> In which I had abandoned the true way.*

It is said that when you arrive in the great beyond, the question posed to you will not be, "Why were you not more like Einstein, Moses, or Ghandi?" Rather, the question will be, "Why were you not more like *you*?" If you find yourself standing in the dark forest, unsure which path is the right one, unsure which path is the authentic version of you, then it's safe to say you have lost a sense of wonder.

We live in a world that dispenses information like candy, except we've been largely exposed to false information and have suffered for it. It's time to break free and pursue our potential. A 2016 study by the Bureau of Labor found that thirty million US workers already have the skills to boost their annual earnings by 70 percent.† What is stopping them from taking this positive step? Too many people can't see the countless possibilities in their future and end up selling themselves and the world short of their life's purpose. At some point, agency and zeal were surrendered, and a poverty mindset took hold. Why?

---

* Dante Alighieri, 1265–1321. *The Divine Comedy of Dante Alighieri: Inferno, Purgatory, Paradise.* New York: The Union Library Association, 1935.

† Steve Lohr, "Up to 30 Million in US Have the Skills to Earn 70% More, Researchers Say," *New York Times*, December 3, 2020, https://www.nytimes.com/2020/12/03/technology/work-skills-upward-mobility.html.

A message has permeated our lives growing up. It was told to us by teachers in grade school, in the plots of movies, in inspirational PSAs from celebrities, and even by our own parents: "Get a degree in a subject you love, and the rest will follow." Though most people have good intentions while giving this directive, they have it all wrong.

Culture perpetuates a belief that you are not capable or qualified unless deemed so by an expert. For some things, of course, credentials are necessary, but on the whole, this myth limits a vision of what is possible. It influences your identity by reducing what opportunities you believe are available. Under this misguided thinking, you feel you have a limited amount of skills and, therefore, a limited amount of opportunities in life.

German philosopher Arthur Schopenhauer solidified this truth when he wrote, "Every man takes the limits of his own field of vision for the limits of the world."* When others influence your vision, you prevent an awareness of what your life could be. Unfortunately, myths perpetuated by culture have inhibited our ability to successfully navigate the modern, ever-changing world by putting our potential, best self in prison.

For those of us who bought that myth, we may suffer from anxiety, emotional claustrophobia, or any combination

---

* Arthur Schopenhauer, *Studies in Pessimism: A Series of Essays* (London: George Allen & Company, Ltd., 1913), 69.

INTRODUCTION

of factors working against our ability to live our lives audaciously. Rather than pursue our true interests, we are in a go-nowhere life, feeling like a cornered animal. What's worse is that most of us in this situation hold the incorrect belief that there are very few options to attain something better.

And why would we believe otherwise? We might think that anything unique or innovative has already been done. So, we might as well remain in the status quo. We all want a direction in life, ideally one that follows our passions and interests. Rarely, though, are we shown how we can pursue what is truly possible.

That's where this book comes in. This is not a manual that will solve all your problems. Instead, it gives you the tools necessary for exploring your ambitions and embracing discovery, adventure, and personal growth through engaging in worder. It gives you permission to succeed.

Everyone has untapped "superpowers" that will allow you to explore and achieve more than you currently believe is in your realm of possibility. How do you jumpstart that process? Well, you need to let go of cultural myths and then formulate a plan with rational underpinnings on the right side of facts. But before that, you must recognize the importance of moving onward at all times. By facing your fears, you allow yourself to evolve by failing into progress.

A CLEAR DIRECTION FORWARD

We all have personal stories of failure. But somewhere along the way, we were taught that failure was a bad thing. That we should strive for anything but failure. Failed tests. Failed courses. Failed projects. Failed relationships. These outcomes are to be shunned and avoided. This type of thinking, of course, is ludicrous and dangerous. The truth is that these "failure" experiences are essential. Without them, we could never grow into our successes. Failure can be seen as feedback, or a learning experience, on the path forward to success.

We've been failing our entire lives, from the time we started walking, talking, and playing sports. I'll spare you from listing all of my failures, but I will share one that may be helpful. In 2007, I had been hauling merchandise in my company van. Driving home to Texas from New Mexico, I arrived in the early hours of the morning, exhausted from the journey. I parked in the driveway and sat there for a few moments to reflect when suddenly it hit me. I felt that my business was going under, and I didn't know how to stop it from happening. My mind scrambled with scenarios on how to fix the situation. Soon, the tears started flowing.

With three children and a fourth on the way, my wife and kids didn't deserve to experience the consequences if I should fail. The weight of the world was on my shoulders, and it was crushing me. I had no blueprint to give me the

INTRODUCTION

answer. As often happens when we lose a clear direction, I asked myself, *How did I get here?*

Up until then, I had been successful. My company created programming for independent television stations in El Paso, Texas, and Las Cruces, New Mexico. Through our programming, we sold gift certificates for things like ski trips and hotel stays at discounted rates. It had worked well for quite some time. Looking to expand, I came up with my next idea. *Why not try a live television auction?* I purchased wholesale and liquidated merchandise—eighteen-wheeler truckloads of merchandise from trusted retailers like Target. I didn't realize that buying, moving, warehousing, inventorying, and selling my own varied merchandise was way more complicated than I expected.

Exacerbating the problem, expenses were too high. I borrowed a large sum of money to purchase the merchandise—money I now was uncertain I could earn back. Additionally, I had just caught an employee stealing from me on video. The sting of betrayal was a new and difficult experience. Was this business losing money because of employee theft, mismanagement, or lack of revenue? It was difficult to know. The only thing I did know was this business wasn't working the way I had intended it to.

Sitting in my driveway with tears rolling down my face, I had to make a choice. The questions were swirling in my mind: *Is this what I really want? Do I double down and make it work? Is this my real purpose? Is this best for my family?*

How do I take care of my investors who trusted me with their money? That's when I realized I had to sell my business to pay off my debts and pursue something more meaningful. But I still felt like a failure.

I took a deep breath, stepped out of the vehicle, and went inside my home, knowing I needed to change my life's direction. It would start by failing forward. This painful moment was actually one of the catalysts that influenced my current progress. By creating a business from scratch, I learned many important things, including how to run a business, how to be confident, how to network, how to seek out mentors in a specific field, how to grow an idea, and how to build relationships with investors. I also learned that experience is the springboard for creating expertise. The most important lesson of all? Following ambition outweighs the cost of failing. Therefore, failing became a necessary component to my success.

My failures, just like yours, are teaching moments and opportunities. Each failure is a new launching pad in a longer, more ambitious adventure to an exciting destination not yet known.

BE ADVENTUROUS

When you bring a sense of wonder and adventure to the possibilities in your future, your experiences will shape the skills you need to grow. You can become the type of person who

INTRODUCTION

changes your immediate circle and then the world. Education and learning are two things I am passionate about. So my next steps were to help develop and found a school. I felt confident that I could do it and do it well. My ability to guide the project to success sprung from skills acquired through my previous business experience. I never doubted myself when creating that school because it was simple compared to what I had gone through before.

In that school's library was a copy of one of my favorite children's books, *Harold and the Purple Crayon*, which illustrates that you bring into existence your own reality through desire and imagination. Harold creates his entire world through his purple crayon. At one point, he accidentally squiggles an ocean, which he immediately falls into. The narrator explains that "Harold was in over his head" but "came up thinking fast." Harold quickly draws a sailboat, climbs in, and sets sail. The narrator says, "After he had sailed long enough, Harold made land without much trouble."* As the book unfolds, more accidental circumstances repeat Harold's penchant for failing forward. He continues to draw new adventures that present problems. In turn, they lead him to new solutions. That is what an adventure looks like: wading into the unknown and learning along the way.

---

* Crockett Johnson, *Harold and the Purple Crayon* (New York: HarperCollins, 2015), 16–21.

If you really want to succeed, you need to carry your own "purple crayon" and create those experiences. You grow by pushing yourself bit by bit into a new adventure (or venture), one you may be unsure you can accomplish. As you move forward, you will create the solutions to the problems that present themselves. If you fall into the proverbial ocean, you will draw your own boat to keep you afloat.

Driving home to Texas from New Mexico, I was like Harold falling into the ocean. When I walked through the front door of my house to change my life, I made land without trouble, full of wonder and ready to start the next adventure. Over the years, my collection of experiences has given me the opportunity to explore and succeed in a wide range of areas. Much of that success was accomplished without me coming to the table as an "expert."

The aim of this book is to help you acquire the same state of mind. You will discover your ambitions and learn to seek them out adventurously. You will have tons of fun, lots of excitement, and wind up wildly more inspired, fulfilled, and successful than you initially thought possible.

IMAGINATION IN MOTION

Ambitions and intentions are more readily and consistently accomplished through putting yourself in motion and staying in motion. Push yourself, bit by bit, toward building your ideas into reality.

INTRODUCTION

In the Declaration of Independence, the second paragraph famously begins, "We hold these truths to be self-evident." However, prior to that document, the ideas contained within were anything but self-evident, and the American colonists' need for the document in the first place is proof. Yet those are ideas that are now self-evident. Truths don't become apparent until you put the dream and its values into action. To do something that hasn't been done yet by others requires you to put in the hard work, the perspiration.

In other words, you need to do your best to adopt the idea often quoted by Reid Hoffman, who described an entrepreneur as somebody who jumps off of a cliff and builds the plane on the way down.* Redevelop the resilience of your imagination and then put it into practice. Pursuing new ideas, companies, and interests adventurously, whether full time or on the side, is crucial to living a wondrous life.

THE WONDER EFFECT

What is *The Wonder Effect*? I define it as the deliberate use of curiosity and optimism to chart a new direction and course for your life, one that you want deep down. The upcoming pages will demonstrate how to ignite your passions and

---

* Drake Baer, "How LinkedIn's Reid Hoffman Jumped Off a Cliff and Built an Airplane," *Fast Company*, May 17, 2013, https://www.fastcompany.com/3009831/how-linkedins-reid-hoffman-jumped-off-a-cliff-and-built-an-airplane.

pursue your calling by moving forward with a sense of wonder. You will use this book to craft a new frame of mind, one that embraces adventure and is willing to learn openly and confidently.

In Chapters 1 and 2, you will unlearn the problems stemming from groupthink while learning how to reconnect with your naturally curious self. Here, you will understand that you are not bound to do what everyone else is being told they must do. What the experts say is good for the collective may not always be good for you as an individual. Without thoughtfully questioning the unseen systems that guide these myths, a synthetic environment will put limitations on what you consider a possibility to explore.

With these false idols crushed, you are free to get to know yourself again. You might not be happy with what you see, but that dissatisfaction is actually a good thing and can act as the catalyst for open-mindedness. Knowing yourself once again, you can transform the diverse set of your life's patches into a quilt of wonder.

From Chapters 3 through 7, you will go through the practical side of *The Wonder Effect*, which includes setting goals through an intentional curriculum. In the process, you will be mindful of choosing the tools that carve the new you by seeking mentorship and putting in the time, effort, and energy needed to fuel your growth, progress, and success.

With the curriculum in place, you will then practice exploration, which can often be fraught with apprehension.

INTRODUCTION

To combat this angst, you will come to understand that putting one foot in front of the other while in pursuit of an envisioned future can bring into existence what you once thought impossible.

From there, you will add an adventurous spirit while building a compass to orient you as an aid for your long-term growth. As you will see, becoming adventurous includes creating space for serendipity, practicing the extraordinary, and overcoming imposter syndrome. Oh, yes, the dreaded imposter syndrome. The persistent inability to believe that one's success is deserved or achieved as the result of one's own efforts or skills. For quite some time, I was filled with imposter syndrome while writing this, but I pushed ahead to construct something I believe is worth sharing. And my hope is that you pass on these ideas with those you know who are inhibited and still looking for permission to succeed at *anything*.

Punctuating these chapters is the obstacle that holds most of us back from taking action: the fear of failure. Failure will be reframed and redefined for you, and changing your perspective on the concept couldn't come sooner. It is the riskiest time in human history to do the safe thing. In the end, you will discover that persistence is one of the keys to stopping your inhibitions from standing in your way.

And finally, in Chapter 8, you will learn the importance of giving back to others. Where many see giving back as just a kind thing to do, or something that you can do once you have "arrived," you will learn it is actually the very thing that energizes your entire life. Like a wondrous cycle, giving back is a source of purpose, acting as the hub and catalyst to do all that you want to do.

In Hebrew, the word *ma'aser*, which you usually translate as "tithing," means "to give 10 percent of your earnings to charity." But it also shares the same root as the word *wealthy*. This play on words has been used to teach that giving and contributing to others is something that also contributes to our own inner wealth, and especially our emotional wealth. When you make a positive impact on the world, you generate feelings of connection and purpose. One might think that it is counterintuitive to become wealthy from giving. But as you'll learn, your generosity is imperative to you pushing yourself beyond what you thought you were capable of accomplishing.

You have choices in front of you. Don't assume that something is beyond your grasp; even if you don't attain it at first, you will have stretched yourself through the pursuit, inching ever closer until you can reach out and grab your dreams.

My hope for you is that you finish the last page with a new capacity to explore your future in an exciting, emotionally fulfilling, and adventurous way. Included in this is gaining the emotional room to breathe and the belief that you can accomplish your stepping-stone goals on the way to a larger

INTRODUCTION

vision. Give yourself permission to pursue your calling with passion, and experience success beyond your wildest dreams.

It is time to stop viewing yourself from the perspective that has been imprinted on you. Allow yourself to have fun, be adventurous, try new things, and unlock new dimensions of yourself that you haven't had access to in years—or ever! This will happen when you begin exploring new opportunities with wondrous possibility, passion, openness, and a desire to pursue your calling.

Welcome to *The Wonder Effect*.

CHAPTER 1

CRUSH FALSE IDOLS

An expert is one who knows more and more about less and less until he knows absolutely everything about nothing.

—NICHOLAS BUTLER

Let's talk about a guy who bet a million dollars against the housing industry and won. In late 2007, the vast majority of financial experts believed there was no cause for alarm in the housing market. However, investor Michael Burry disagreed. Not only did he believe the housing market would fail; he believed that short-selling—selling the current market value with a promise to buy back at a lower value—was an opportunity to financially profit from the inevitable crash. Experts thought his analysis was preposterous. *The market could not crash*, the collective thought. Well, as history would have it, a wave of experts went bankrupt, and Burry personally made $100 million. His fund saw

$700 million in earnings. He saw something that the experts didn't, probably because he had no need to be validated by them. It was such a significant moment in international economic history that Burry's story was depicted in the film *The Big Short*.

You may be thinking, *Isn't Michael Burry also an expert?* As mentioned, the underlying difference between him and everyone else is that he looked at the housing market with open eyes while using his own creativity to gather facts. He did not nod along with the echo chamber of groupthink. When you do the work to understand a situation, as Michael Burry did, and use first principles to analyze, you stand at a higher vista to see farther and more clearly than single-minded, self-assured experts. This requires you to set aside false idols and trust yourself. What is a false idol? Anyone you assume embodies a sense of power or perfection that they actually don't possess but are often *attributed* with those characteristics by others who put them on a pedestal.

FROM LEARN TO EARN

Let's unpack the situation to see how Burry's hard work overcame the industry experts and reshaped how we think about housing bubbles. How did Burry apply new critical thinking? In part, Burry used basic principles associated with behavioral economics to learn things others couldn't see. Everyone else, on the other hand, used traditional economics. In traditional economics, we understand consumer behavior to be logical and well-informed. Housing "experts" using traditional economics saw the spike of predatory loans and could not anticipate the negative consequences due to their limited scope. They assumed consumers taking these loans were knowledgeable and took thoughtful consideration to any risks before signing the deal. They assumed that consumers, as logical players in a logical economy, would make every effort to follow through on payments and exhibit fiduciary responsibility, as most consumers had done before. There were many assumptions made, and the problem with assumptions is that they prevent you from thinking more deeply than you otherwise would. The effect is a type of blindness to what may be in front of you, which is exacerbated when you are incentivized to have certain conclusions. So, these experts did not critically think through the situation.

What did these experts not see? First, the loans themselves were written to undermine a consumer's capacity for well-informed decisions, hence their post-crash description as "predatory." They also wrongly believed that due to the vast size of the market, it could not fail, which was obviously not true.

Burry's favor for behavioral economics allowed him to peel apart the underlying reasons for the traditionalist assumptions. In one application of behavioral economics, the strength of a consumer's purchasing power and the economy overall are dictated by the principles of reach and psychology.

Let's unpack the idea of reach and psychology in behavioral economics by comparing an NFL player and a public-school teacher. Why is a professional athlete paid millions of dollars in annual salary while the mind-shaping educator earns what can generously be described as a living wage? The short answer is that an NFL player can reach and influence millions of people each year; whereas a teacher may reach thirty a year—if the students are paying attention.

With a larger reach, more consumers are influenced. That's when psychology comes in. Because of an NFL player's larger consumer reach, fans of the player psychologically feel like they belong to a community that confirms and legitimizes their admiration of this player. To signal that they belong to this group of supporters, they are willing to spend money to confirm their belonging to that collective. By buying and wearing an NFL player jersey—an economy-boosting purchase of $120 a pop—a fan has a high chance of having that purchase psychologically confirmed as a reasonable one. That Sunday while watching the big game, a like-minded person will give that jersey-wearer a nod of approval, confirming the behavioral motivation that led to the consumer's purchase.

The reason you don't see people buying and wearing replicas of their favorite teacher's sweater and cheering from the hallways is because—with around nine hundred total

CRUSH FALSE IDOLS

students served over a thirty-year period—there is very little chance a given consumer will run into somebody with mutual admiration for that specific teacher. Our inner voice tells us something like this: *No. Buying my favorite teacher's replica sweater will not get my psychological needs met.* The teacher's reach is smaller; therefore the psychology of the consumer changes. The economy then works itself out and notices it can pay people differently based on how each earner can influence marketable action.

Bringing this back to Burry, he wanted to figure out the underlying behavioral reasons and consequences of the loans entering the market. Asking unique questions about reach and psychology gave him the ability to learn what was really behind the choices of bankers and home buyers and why that would tank the market.

His answers were simple. Bankers, with their deep pockets for lending, can reach nearly any household. That's quite the reach. Psychologically, the increase of subprime loans gave lenders a win-win: money from the high interest rates *or* the title of the foreclosed house if the loan went south. At the micro level, certain banks—who settled with the federal government and admitted no wrongdoing—encouraged individual employees to accumulate as many predatory loans as possible via internal policies and commissions-based pay.

For homebuyers, the chance to own a home despite having weak finances was dangled in front of them like bait and offered an easy gateway to upward economic mobility.

Prospective homeowners would misstate their income in order to qualify for the better-than-belief loan, something that, ordinarily, a bank would investigate and use to stop the loan—protecting the finances of all parties. However, lenders were incentivized to create more and more loans. In the end, many banks knowingly looked the other way. Over time, the accumulation of these financial improprieties added up and caused the system to fail.

How did "expert" groupthink create a tunnel vision that ignored evidence of a market headed for disaster? The facts were actually pretty obvious, but nobody wanted to acknowledge them. Nearly everyone's livelihood—bankers, brokers, investors, homeowners, and more—depended on the housing market. It wasn't just the homeowners and lenders who fomented the situation. The investors on Wall Street selling the loans and then selling bets on those packages were affected too. So much of the financial world was tied up in the housing market that when it failed, it was going to fail big. They didn't have the capacity to see that it would fail because of simple greed; plus, they didn't want it to fail.

Financial experts in their echo chamber began a collective internal dialogue that may have sounded something like this: *If everyone else is doing this, and they've been doing this for a couple of years now, it can't be so bad. Let's continue to write these loans! We'll just pass the buck to the consumer if things get a little hairy. But it's okay because nothing's blown*

CRUSH FALSE IDOLS

up yet. Their expertise in the situation was a misguided, myopic hope rather than an innovative, critical look at all of the facts. A full perspective requires 360 degrees. When everyone is pointed in a singular direction, there are 359 other directions being ignored. One reason you need to be wary of groupthink, like Burry, is to generate a full range of perspectives of your life's direction.

Side-stepping the tunnel vision of expert groupthink is the first order of business in *The Wonder Effect*. There is no capacity for curious exploration when you are following behind people on a narrow path. In order to act on your own, you need to think for yourself, be willing to experiment on your own terms, and question unverified or assumed information. This process begins by closely examining experts and then yourself in a thoughtful way, as we will explore throughout this chapter. Doing so helps you determine what information is parroted in an echo chamber or, alternatively, uses hard facts and critical thinking. When groupthink sets in, external factors unrelated to the facts create a kind of tunnel vision that obscures the whole story. Those ensnared in groupthink begin to undermine their own potential for ambitious and thoughtful action outside of the narrow narrative they've burrowed themselves into. Henry David Thoreau said it perfectly: "Think for yourself, or others will think for you without thinking of you."

A crucial difference between groupthink and true expertise is reasoning using complete and holistic evidence. Many facts can and should be collectively agreed upon, but here we are talking about systems driven by conjecture, anecdotal evidence, or otherwise uncritically examined structures. When a thought process is built on these shaky premises, it can be difficult to break free from the many inherent mistakes they contain.

Yes, even the so-called experts can make mistakes, as Burry discovered. He turned his own analytical skills into a successful financial situation. He learned, and then he earned. So when you find yourself in an environment that doesn't fully analyze things in a critical and unapologetic way, and is on the wrong side of the facts, how do you shake loose from groupthink?

FOLLOW THE ROADS NOT TAKEN

Shedding groupthink requires you to complete two fundamental steps. First, you must find appropriate resources. What does that mean? As a thought experiment, let's think of our parental figures. Although we often go to our parents for direction, as we genuinely should, they may not be the appropriate resource for all topics. For instance, asking most parents for advice about working on blockchain or NFTs is probably a bad idea not just because they will have a confused, generational-gap look on their face, but also because they simply haven't been around long enough to be informed. Instead, one

CRUSH FALSE IDOLS

should read, explore, and have conversations with anyone involved, even in tangential ways, in those technologies.

Finding an appropriate resource is not enough though. As it pertains to the 2008 housing crisis, we can now say with some confidence that anyone vetting their own investments through lenders, financial experts, and everybody on Wall Street seemed like the appropriate resources to utilize. To safeguard against this possibility, we need to follow up with the second step.

For step two, you must evaluate if your resources are valuable—even if they seem legitimate—by determining if they have 1) experience, not just knowledge, 2) a holistic and diverse set of facts and tools, and 3) humility. What do I mean by humility? That means the resource conveys what they are not certain about and welcomes innovative ideas, approaches, and systems to their field.

One way you can spot myopic groupthink is if the so-called expert offers very little variability in their answers and is trying to push you (and everyone else) in one direction. A lower-stakes occurrence of this myopic phenomenon occurs with high school guidance counselors. Although they are well-meaning and do quite a bit of good in the world, they offer students somewhat limited advice. When advising the student interested in programming smartphone apps, the guidance counselor might say, "Go to *this* college, which has an excellent computer programming degree." To the student with dreams of becoming an actor, they might say, "Go to *this* college, which has an excellent acting program." For the student with dreams of becoming a chef, they say, "Go to *this* vocational school, which has an excellent cooking program." "Go to college," it seems, is the only answer they give. Surely there are other options available to high school students besides college, but they may never know. Somewhere along the way, a social myth to go to college emerged. Guidance counselors became ensnared in the myth and were trained that college was *the* answer to any and all student interests. And this limited viewpoint grossly undermines the potential of students who have countless other avenues to explore their interests.

This type of single-minded thinking in guidance counseling was also at play prior to the 2008 recession. Because he crushed false idols, Michael Burry avoided the singular thinking of the financial world. Instead, he acted into expertise to become a *real* expert. It wasn't so much that Burry had a crystal ball or got lucky. Quite the opposite. He took paths that the experts did not, looking at sound and foundational economic principles but applying them in a different way.

Burry took the roads not taken. In Robert Frost's famous poem "The Road Not Taken," it implies that there are only two roads: one taken frequently and one hardly taken. In fact, there are hundreds if not thousands of roads not taken, and you have the capacity to clear the path and be the first

CRUSH FALSE IDOLS

one down a truly innovative road. The only limits to your progress are the limits of your imagination. Most people deemed an expert—seeing only one or two roads—lack a certain perspective and imagination that successful people have.

To paraphrase James Altucher: There is no one path. There is every path, and every path starts with this moment. What does that mean, really? It means that in order to shed the dangers of groupthink and become *real* experts, you need to cultivate your own experiences.

There are, of course, some narrow paths, such as becoming a doctor, that require much tighter oversight. Doctors require specific training and education. They must go to medical school, become board certified and licensed, and complete their specialization in a residency program. However, you could enter the health and wellness industry—an industry that is growing tremendously—through other means. For example, Tony Robbins teamed up with Peter Diamandis, MD, to own and operate a healthcare firm that focuses on preventative care in favor of the reactive care that dominates the industry.

Most interests and professions don't require the educational rigor of becoming a physician. And you could grow into an expert for multiple professional fields. Just look at Elon Musk. His degree was in physics, which explains some of his career trajectory, but he didn't let that prevent him from exploring all of his options. His first business enterprise developed online city maps and yellow pages. Then, with no formal training in finance, he founded an online finance company that eventually merged with and became PayPal. Despite no training in city infrastructure, Musk's The Boring Company has found success building transportation and tunnels for cities across the world. Further in the world of transportation, his companies Tesla and SpaceX have become pretty well-known for revolutionizing the car and space industries. But stop to think about that. A single man with no formal training was able to turn two long-standing American institutions on their head. Elsewhere, Musk is leading businesses innovating AI, music, social media, and, of all things, perfume. What you can discern from Elon Musk is that there is no single avenue to finding your way into the life you want to lead. Pursue your interests for yourself rather than the expectations of groupthink.

That is what Kurt Warner did. If you are unaware of Warner, he is an NFL quarterback with MVP, Super Bowl champion, and Hall of Famer on his résumé. The traditional and typically singular path to the NFL is to be drafted out of college. Warner went undrafted, then he defied expectations. Continuing to pursue his ambitions, he signed with an Arena Football team, the Iowa Barnstormers. There, he grew and flourished as a player for two years. This led to a "futures contract" with the NFL Europe team Amsterdam Admirals, where he went on to lead the league in passing and touchdowns. These three years of experiences led to an NFL contract and the "greatest show on turf" that he is now known for today. Warner went on his own unique path outside of groupthink expectations.

Because groupthink suggests there are only a few paths forward, many are not adequately prepared for an inevitably unpredictable future. Like Harold from *Harold and the Purple Crayon*, the future wields its own purple crayon that could, at any moment, squiggle an ocean underneath you. However, there are skills—discussed throughout this book—to improve your chances for success in the future that involve attenuating your own thought processes and developing a healthy skepticism to what everyone is saying.

Ultimately, the combination of these skills is what I call *The Wonder Effect*. Why that name? In its simplest form, it means that if you simply wonder what is possible and pull the thread of that wonder, you will pursue actions that create direct or indirect results of positive growth. When you internalize, *What would happen if . . . ?* or, *I wonder if . . . ?* or any variation of those, you will tug slightly on any interest that may make you a little bit more fulfilled to see where it goes. Just wonder what could be. Have a purple crayon.

FUTURE CAST YOURSELF

Interested in the way in which experts influence us, psychologist Philip Tetlock got to work. In his seminar "Why Foxes Are Better Forecasters Than Hedgehogs," Tetlock revealed research about the accuracy and reliability of expert prediction in a long-term study.* He solicited twenty-eight thousand forecasted predictions from 284 experts who were deemed qualified to make the solicited opinions. Decades later, when he could compare actual results to the predictions, Tetlock tried to see if any specific types of experts—liberal compared to conservative, optimistic compared to pessimistic, among many other opposing traits—were better at predicting than other groups. The only pattern that emerged was *how* the experts structured their thinking.

He found that those who gave their predictions confidently and singularly (without alternatives or "howevers"), were not only wrong more often but would also make excuses for why the results differed from their predictions. Additionally, Tetlock argued that their style of rhetoric seemed to be designed to annoy those who disagreed with them. He called this group "hedgehogs" because, apparently, hedgehogs act similarly confident and singular in nature.

On the other hand, the most accurate expert predictions had a more holistic and open style. They demonstrated skepticism when it came to one or two grand theories, offered many alternatives, showed an openness to adjusting their line of thinking, based their ideas on facts and evidence, and

---

* Stewart Brand, "Philip Tetlock, Why Foxes Are Better Forecasters Than Hedgehogs," *The Long Now Foundation,* January 26, 2007, https://longnow.org/seminars/02007/jan/26/why-foxes-are-better-forecasters-than-hedgehogs/.

offered their predictions with modesty. Tetlock termed this group "foxes," as foxes tend to behave more thoughtfully and with less surety in nature.

Unlike the hedgehogs, the foxes' predictions weren't designed to target a specific and opposing ideology or political viewpoint. Instead, their predictions tended to be unfavorable to and undermine all ideologies across the spectrum. These experts also admitted when they were wrong. In other words, reliable experts are more open, holistic, honest, and interested in the facts.

Of course, timidness and thoughtfulness doesn't get a lot of airtimes on cable news or reality TV that privileges conflict and chaos. Because hedgehogs dominate the conversation and are the most visible experts, many of our policies, cultural myths, and underlying systems are being built and sustained by people who are wrong more often than the word *expert* would imply.

A further takeaway from Tetlock is that there is an inverse relationship between fame and accuracy. In other words, the more famous a person becomes for their expertise, the less likely they are to have their ideas put through checks and balances. These factors cause their predictions to be as accurate as chance.

Approach anybody you solicit advice from with a question mark. When their advice is appropriate, offers a holistic experience, is based in sound analysis, and isn't the easy way out, they are likely pointing you in the right direction.

The easy way out—soliciting the singular answer—is tempting but often wrong. I learned this lesson when I took a correspondence economics course to finish my high school diploma. The instructor sent me the study guide for the final exam, and it was a pittance. To help guide me, I went to an appropriate resource: the economics teacher at my high school familiar with the textbook. When I met with him to ask for the key to passing the exam, hoping he'd give me a CliffsNotes version, he told me to read the whole textbook assigned for the course and make the effort to learn all of its content. "If you do that, you'll be fine," he said. This was absolutely the right advice, but there was a part of me that wanted an easy way out.

If he wouldn't give me the CliffsNotes version, perhaps he could highlight specific core things that would appear on the exam. If that had happened, I would have likely passed the exam, but I would not have learned anything nor received an experience to help generate expertise. Because I absorbed the entire textbook, my interest in its content and wanting to adventurously question its content spurred my interest in finance and running my own business, which makes up part of my successes today. I had to experience the textbook's subject matter for myself to earn my expertise. If the teacher had short-cutted the answers straight into my hand and I accepted, it would have been like me giving away my own autonomy.

CRUSH FALSE IDOLS

When you have experiences for yourself, you are better able to be on the right side of facts, which, in turn, lets you forecast the future—or, more accurately, to futurecast. To manifest this, you need to imaginatively explore a new version of yourself, casting that into the future. Creating this vision will help you take those steps to realize this new you. It's almost like writing a fictionalized novel of yourself and then creating your life toward that fiction.

Someone's internalized dialogue might look like this: *I am an accountant in an industrialized city, but I love the water and wildlife of Alaska. If I owned a fish distribution company, I could love a life of being on the seas.* Filling in the details of this Alaska-version of themselves will help them connect to the steps to make the transition. Their life choices will backfill once their future self is known. The gap between where they are now and where they want to go, as well as skills transferred, will be explored by the rest of the book's concepts. As a former accountant, they should easily be able to run a business.

Keep in mind, I'm not saying that being an accountant is a bad endeavor. It's a perfectly good profession, but it wasn't the right fit for that hypothetical individual. It's not a loser-to-winner situation. They were successful before. It's winner-to-different. Additionally, futurecasting need not be relegated to one's profession. It can be as incremental, small, or as big of a lifestyle change as desired. Change could be motivated by burnout, pursuing a new interest, implementing one's desired lifestyle, or anything else.

If, instead of futurecasting, you instead are influenced by groupthink experts, the way you forecast your future is often on the wrong side of facts, as Tetlock showed.

THE WRONG SIDE OF FACTS

Economist and *Freakonomics* coauthor Steven D. Levitt has made it his purpose to study facts. For him, factual information can be an olive branch of opportunity or a hammer that smashes critical thought. Interested in the latter, Levitt's work reflects our society and how its damaging policies are not remediated to accurately reflect reality. Because he is a behavioral economist, he primarily focuses on policies that have a dangerous or negative impact on our lives.

One of his most famous findings concerns automobile car seats for children.* In the United States, children under five years of age are required by law to ride in a car seat. That law seems to be the direct opposite of factual reality. Car seats are the most dangerous restraint option for children over two years old. The policy's well-meaning mistake is motivated by a cultural myth and stigma: anybody who would

---

* Steven Levitt, "Surprising Stats About Child Car Seats," filmed July 2005, at TEDGlobal 2005, Oxford, UK, TED video, 18:45, https://www.ted.com/talks/steven_levitt_surprising_stats_about_child_carseats?language=en.

refuse a car seat for their two-year-old child (or older) must be a child endangerer. Levitt's research shows there is no proven benefit for using a car seat for children ages two and up. And he used the US government's own published data on the National Highway Safety Administration's website from 1975 to mid-2005 (the time of his initial report).

The only metric in which the car seat (barely) outperformed the lap-and-shoulder belt was in head-on crashes. Levitt proposed that because seat manufacturers are only compelled to test their product safety through head-on testing, the products are designed to perform well in that specific type of accident. However, for every other type of crash (such as side-impact or rear-impact crashes), the car seats perform worse than the lap-and-shoulder belt.

Curiously, when Levitt commissioned his own crash tests to collect additional data, most testing companies denied his request. They were afraid that their association with Levitt and the findings themselves would interfere with established business connections and revenue with seat manufacturers. The only company that did agree only did so under the condition of anonymity.

Levitt's commissioned test found that lap-and-shoulder seat belts could pass government regulations designed for child car seats serving children two years old and older. Yet the US government and their deemed experts have maintained that the law should stand, using mostly anecdotal testimonials from parents and the influence of lobbyists. These anecdotes transform into social myths—myths that sound eerily similar to old groupthink: "You have to go to college to succeed." That dangerous social myths dictate policy instead of data-informed decision-making occurs very often, endangering innovation and undermining critical thinking.

So, the car-seat law purports to limit danger to our children, but it actually does the opposite. The wrong-side-of-facts logic, experienced by the average consumer, sounds something like this: "The government wouldn't be telling me to use these car seats if this weren't the safest option." This surface-level faith in experts causes us to slip into the unimaginative environment of groupthink.

Why isn't the lap-and-shoulder belt legal if it passes the tests? Why isn't an even safer system designed? The answer, of course, is connected to the fact that, in the United States alone, child car seats fetch nearly $1 billion in annual sales. The truth would hurt their industry.

Is the law designed for the parents' and children's best interests, or for the manufacturers'? Wouldn't having an additional billion dollars to spend on their children in other ways be an important lifeline for parents raising their children? Perhaps, like those tied to the housing market in 2008, the reliance on car seat sales has become too large to fail for some, and now many in the industry are lobbying to keep it going.

Ultimately, the car-seat law as it applies to two-year-old children and older is a governmental policy not informed by data, facts, and information but instead by the wrong side of facts. It represents the truth that social myths mislead informed decision-making. When facts no longer become the basis by which decisions are made, so-called experts create synthetic environments that prop up systems that inherently undermine us. When accepting these environments at face value, it caps our potential and stifles our direction. Instead of dwelling in social myths and synthetic environments, you need to cultivate a more nuanced reality.

THE DANGERS OF SYNTHETIC REALITIES

Operating within synthetic realities limits our growth potential. The story of the common goldfish demonstrates this principle. The goldfish will grow depending on their environment. When placed in a small fishbowl, a goldfish maintains its small size and, if well fed, sees a lifespan of a few weeks to three years. Considering the potential of a goldfish, a small-bowl fate envelops and inhibits their growth.

If, on the other hand, the goldfish is placed in an adequately sized living environment that gives them the chance to explore and move freely in any direction, they can grow up to one foot in length. Have you ever heard of a foot-long goldfish before? It's difficult to even imagine because of the normalized narrative of the tiny goldfish in the tiny bowl. When given a large tank, they can grow to their full potential and live up to twenty or thirty years. That means the synthetic environment pet culture has perpetuated prevents goldfish from living 90 percent of their potential life.

Living in the synthetic reality of expert groupthink is similar to a goldfish living in a tiny fishbowl. For those inhibited by social myths, you are a goldfish that may be living in a tiny fishbowl. This signals an important dilemma you must face. You need to ask yourself these questions: *Am I living in a synthetic environment? If so, how is it inhibiting my growth?*

As individuals, it is far too easy to slip into social myths, such as the myth that everybody should go to college. And let me just say that I am in favor of learning and education. But as individuals, the selection of options should not be automatic. Always analyze your situation after attenuating your own thought processes and developing a healthy skepticism to what everyone is saying.

One day my daughter came home enamored with going to a specific college. In the process of looking to me for direction, we started doing some research to begin the critical-thinking process. It turned out that her number-one college was $70,000 a year in tuition alone. Not including the expenses of housing and food, upon graduation, she would enter the job market with $280,000 of debt. Excluding loan interest rates or the huge burden debt puts on cash flow—which undermines future investment opportunities—I could not see how this huge amount of debt outweighed other potentials for the cash required for the degree. Simply investing that total amount in real estate or the equities market could very easily, in four years' time, make as much if not more than several decades of earnings from the job that the degree helped acquire.

Learning these details, my daughter decided to do some due diligence. Rather than be blinded by one possible path, she explored others. She found another school that would cost around $15,000 a year for a parallel course of education. I was proud of her for putting herself first and not simply giving in to a system (seemingly) designed to put her at a disadvantage. Yet so many others are often sold the damaging social myth that unaffordable college and the synthetic realities they construct are the *only* path to success.

Colleges create synthetic environments beyond their tendency to cash in on the dreams of their students. In the real world, you deal with a cross-section of the population from all types of backgrounds, ages, and experiences. Yet at the four-year university level, the bulk of the student body is segregated by age and affluence. Freshmen are typically eighteen years old, and the more affluent go to more affluent colleges—and so on down the line. That is not how the real world works. Wall Street traders are not all thirty-five years old, and no one in that field makes the exact same income. How is it that anybody can say a student's experience at college will be similar to their experience in the job market? In terms of environments, college is a tiny fishbowl compared to the ocean of experience.

With car seats or college, groupthink and social myth layer one mistaken belief on top of another until it simply becomes normal, accepted, or sometimes lawfully enforced to start behaving in a way that is on the wrong side of facts. You must do your best to look at these environments with a critical eye to choose what is best for your growth.

If you desire to become wise or successful, you first need to remove any semblance of groupthink that may be invisibly guiding or inhibiting you along the way.

SHED YOUR SKIN

In the natural world, animals shed their outer layer, be it feathers, fur, the exoskeleton, or skin. They do this for one important reason: to grow and increase their ability to thrive. If you are to foster your own growth and ambitiously seek success, you must shed your outer layer of groupthink and social myths. This won't be easy, as groupthink can quickly become a tough and durable layer.

The first step in shedding groupthink is to eliminate the validation you seek from the so-called experts. When you validate the ideas of groupthink, you are giving away your brain to somebody else. Instead, look to primary principles that you should be cultivating for your own growth.

You do not need personal or systemic validation to fulfill your maximum potential. Before finishing my high school diploma, I informed my mom that I would travel abroad. I can still see her reaction of horror. Ultimately, she was terrified I would become a high school dropout. I lacked personal validation from her, and her cause for concern was spurred by the social myth that without a high school diploma, I would become a derelict. In the sense that very few would hire me without a diploma, I was also without social validation to pursue my goals.

But I had a passion for learning beyond the limits of my local high school. If I had sought validation from adult experts who bought into the social myth of the value of a high school diploma, I wouldn't have gone. As Mark Twain said, "Don't let schooling interfere with your education."* And I didn't. I ultimately learned and experienced far more in that year abroad than I otherwise would have had I stayed. My life has been enriched by that choice.

If it wasn't for that decision, I wouldn't have met my wife, I wouldn't have my wonderful kids, and I wouldn't be on the life trajectory that I am on today. And because I have seen successes, I know that it was the most important decision I have ever made; it all started with making a choice to shed my skin and to grow beyond what the experts around me thought they knew.

Leaning into your intuition and listening to your heart might require some practice. First, it's important to know that

---

* Mark Twain Quotes. BrainyQuote.com, BrainyMedia Inc, 2024. https ://www.brainyquote.com/quotes/mark_twain_141715, accessed May 6, 2024.

your intuition offers no certainty or proof that the thing you feel or think is actually correct. You might be wrong, but so might everyone else. But the draw of intellect/heart/intuition is that it is a *signal* to you. It's fine to pursue it and be wrong, but it's better to gain that experience and the knowledge and sense of wisdom from that experience. The intuitive signal should stoke your curiosity because continually stoking this flame, in the long run, will be the best determinant of your success. You can come at this from *curiosity*, not necessarily supernatural knowledge.

Even though I was starting a new adventure into the unknown, my lack of knowledge was accompanied by a purposeful choice to expand my fish tank, so to speak, and to give myself a greater capacity for growth. Going through with my desire to study abroad generated an internal fortitude to thrive in new and unfamiliar situations.

Getting a diploma, in the context of the collective of high schoolers, may be an important step to economic independence. And it is good for the country that everybody is as educated as possible. But in the context of specific individuals, it might not be the best thing for every single person. At that point in time in my life, a diploma wasn't what was best for me. It turns out that what is best for the collective is not necessarily always good for you. And you need to be able to discern when to break from the mold using critical thinking and being on the right side of facts.

CRUSH FALSE IDOLS

WHAT'S BEST FOR THE COLLECTIVE . . .

So why is it that these collective-dictating social myths and policies exist? Quite simply, it's to safekeep the largest number of people possible. Without the idea that we *should* get a diploma, it is likely that very few people would go to school. In short, guiding the collective for their own good ensures social order. Think about how this occurs at the microcosmic level in summer camp. Camps have rules, policies, and unspoken expectations just like broader society. At the start of any given camp day, kids experience a communal breakfast, some activities, and then a break for snack time. Their breakfast might be something nutritional, like oats and eggs, and they reward the kids later after a physical activity with a candy bar during snack time. What if one kid asks their camp counselors for the candy bar at breakfast? Doesn't that break the candy-as-reward mechanism of a system that keeps the kids in line? The camp counselor will decline the candy-desiring child because they have to keep the whole system controlled. If they give this one kid permission to eat candy right away, then the other kids might want candy, and things could descend into chaos rather quickly. Have you ever seen a group of kids experiencing a sugar rush simultaneously? Chaos is not an overexaggeration.

But what if eating oats and eggs is not the best thing for that particular kid? What if this kid needs to start with a candy bar to moderate their blood sugar levels because of hypoglycemia or diabetes? What has been imposed on the collective as best for that group would be detrimental for this individual kid's ability to thrive and stay healthy. These days, medical exceptions would likely be made, but this kind of collective-breaking to serve individuals is a relatively new practice and seldom honored.

Of course, small spats about candy at a summer camp are, in the grand scheme of things, no big deal. But what applies to snack time at camp also applies to federal law. As Levitt discovered with seat belts, the "good for the collective" child seat belt law actually endangers thousands of children each day.

That rules for the collective inhibit the safety and happiness of the individual goes against our—America's—purported pursuit of happiness. Rather than pursue individualism, there is a tendency to design policies and social myths quite like the Borg, the fictional aliens from the *Star Trek* series. Once part of the Borg, any individual member functions to perpetuate sameness and erase individuality. In a way, we are all suffering from living in a world that is dominated by Borg-like structures and perspectives that cater not to you or me as individuals, but to how we should function within a system for the betterment of the whole rather than ourselves. That places a limiting identity on us, a smaller fishbowl that can constrain our growth, shorten the longevity of our feelings of passion and purpose, and crush our imagination and capacity for innovative contributions to society. If our lack of growth leads to depression or other health issues, it may very well limit our capacity for life too.

Say it with me this time: what's best for the collective is not necessarily what's best for you. Make sure you fully consider all of your possibilities—even those that break social myths—and do your due diligence to see if there is another path that is right for you. Then, if you find holistic evidence that supports your perspective, unapologetically follow that path toward your new future.

FIND YOUR OWN EXPERTISE

The impact of finding your own expertise cannot be understated. When you let yourself be dictated by others, it only limits you in minor ways. But sometimes it undermines your basic quality of life. That is what Phillip Stutts found out when he was diagnosed with an incredibly rare disease called achalasia. Those who suffer from this have nerve damage in the esophagus that makes it extremely difficult to swallow. Multiple doctors told him that there was no cure and that within five years he would be eating through a feeding tube.

Rather than take "there is no cure" as the only road by which he could travel, Stutts began to research and look for possible cures. He decided to move forward and cultivate his own expertise. After many rejections, he finally teamed up with doctors at Johns Hopkins University. Early on, he had minor procedures to open up his esophagus to let consumed items travel naturally down, but the nerve damage and inability to swallow persisted. He then attempted revolutionary stem cell procedures.

In a famous blog he wrote after the surgery, he refused to characterize the ineffective procedure as a failure. He concluded his blog by saying he would try again, this time doubling the amount of stem cells injected into the site. Explaining why he didn't accept the procedure as a failure, he wrote, "The only failure is not trying."*

At the time of writing, his disease hasn't been cured yet, but his work has steadily improved his symptoms rather than disable his ability to eat and drink, as his original doctors predicted. Because of Stutt's desire to find his own expertise, achalasia can now be treated successfully. The stem cell treatment was so effective that six months later, he could eat a protein bar without the need for water to wash it down. If he had refused to grow into his own expertise, he'd be eating through a tube by now without the use of his throat.

Rather than settle for what others have told you is normal, you need to read the whole proverbial textbook on your own. You need to be willing to find your own cure, as Stutts is doing. Then analyze the market in a way that others are not, as Burry did. When you become your own expert through experience,

---

* Phillip Stutts, "The Moonshot XII: An Update on My Clinical Trial," PhillipStutts.com, September 18, 2020, https://phillipstutts.com/the-moonshot-xii-an-update-on-my-clinical-trial-by-phillip-stutts/.

this doesn't mean that you are expelling all experts or somehow learning in a vacuum. It means that you seek out those experts who are, as Tetlock would call them, foxes. Utilize those who have experience, an active imagination, and are holistic, open-minded, curious, collaborative, and innovative. Adopt these traits and aim to be a fox yourself. Find a fox and become their apprentice, if possible, to continue learning through experience while your engine runs on curiosity. We will discuss mentorship in more detail in Chapter 3.

Until you can do something yourself, there is usually a large gulf between intellectual knowledge and fully knowing. When learning, experience, and curiosity are fused, *real* expertise is soon to follow. Once you become your own expert, you will be free from the shackles of groupthink. If you are missing one of those three ingredients—learning, experience, and curiosity—you may fall short of what is truly possible for you.

And it's never too late to cultivate yourself. If you want to grow out of your past and beyond the obstacles in your way, you can't rely on the same thinking that has led you to where you are. Using *The Wonder Effect*, lead with curiosity and wonder, decluttering the noise from so-called experts.

CLEAN THE CLUTTER

The important conclusion of crushing the false idolatry of experts—or the misplaced authority and power given to experts—is this: you must filter them out of your headspace. When you shed groupthink, you clear the mental clutter of social myths that have been influencing more of your behavior than you might have realized.

With room to breathe, you have the opportunity to get to know yourself again, freer from outside influence. In that undertaking, and with new space for curiosity and imagination, you will find out who you are, who you have the possibility to become, and the directions you are able to grow. In *Freakonomics*, Steven Levitt argues that despite "spending more time with themselves than with any other person, people often have surprisingly poor insight into their skills and abilities."* It is time to get to know yourself again, or discover new dimensions about yourself that you may have not been in touch with yet.

---

* Steven D. Levitt, *Freakanomics: A Rogue Economist Explores the Hidden Side of Everything* (New York: William Morrow, 2009), 18.

CHAPTER 2

KNOW YOURSELF

My past does not equal my future. Where you go depends entirely on who you choose to be, from this moment on.

—HAL ELROD

Elephants, to put it mildly, are quite large. What's more, they are much larger than their trainers. So, it is curious that we generally don't hear stories about elephants breaking free from their puny trainers and running amok. After all, their capacity to overpower the boundaries of their captivity is obvious. Subduing these gigantic creatures is actually quite involved. Trainers must intervene when the elephants are young and small to mentally condition them that they are too weak to break free.

How this is accomplished is as interesting as it is horrifying. It involves driving a stake into the ground and attaching a small length of rope to the baby elephant. As the baby learns to walk and explore its space, the rope will limit its mobility. As the elephant continues to grow, they accept their limitations as a natural part of their existence. They adopt a fixed mindset that they lack the potential for growth or the ability to change their environment. When they become adults, their limited capacity and underutilized potential become ingrained in them as normal. With this new normal, they submit to a version of themselves that is weak and incapable.

Replace the word *elephant* with *human*, and it would still be a fairly accurate, if metaphorical, representation of people. Like circus elephants, people are trained to develop with certain limitations. For example, we get used to viewing ourselves based on the way other people think about and shape us. When we are younger, and before our talents have emerged or developed, we tend to adopt certain personas. Adults will say things like, "That kid is always such a klutz." They are not always superficially negative. Sometimes it might be, "They are so curious" or "They have always been so organized."

Regardless of the projection, we are trained to believe specific, relegating things that are not necessarily indicative of who we really are or can be. Adopting a limited mindset, we look at ourselves through the eyes of others. In turn, we stop stretching, growing, and pursuing those things that would be fulfilling and quite amazing.

To live life with wonder, however, we need to unlearn the limiting beliefs that have tied us down like the baby elephant's rope and, instead, know ourselves again with a growth mindset that accepts our capacity for change and growth.

THE ELEPHANT IN THE ROOM

By the time people grow into their skills and talents, the direction of that growth has been altered by the many narratives they've been told about the world and about themselves. They may think, *I can't follow my passion for dance because I've always been such a klutz,* and their mind starts to answer every situation the same way: *I can't do that because I am a klutz.*

This invisible training mentally imprisons us to believe we are not capable of many things. When we approach the world with these beliefs, we tend to perpetuate those beliefs in a self-fulfilling prophecy of lost potential. We take on roles, or the aforementioned personas, and perform them. Some are the black sheep. Some are rebels. Some are jocks. Some are studious. Some are Goody Two-shoes. We fulfill them for our friends, family, coworkers, and others because there is something oddly validating about feeling like we have definitive features and attributes. But by maintaining a belief that we belong to a particular label, we prevent our own growth and stop short of knowing and becoming our true selves.

How often do you reflect on those beliefs holding you back? Probably very infrequently. They are so seldom discussed at any level—publicly or interpersonally—that they become the unspoken but obvious object in the room with us, or the proverbial elephant in the room. Unacknowledged limiting beliefs hide our true selves from us.

So how can you know yourself again or see that other dimension? When attributes are imprinted onto you, they hijack you toward achieving that limiting agenda. When you step back and ask yourself deep and meaningful questions that explore *why* you are traveling down your current paths, you may find that you aren't sure. Many have never actually stopped to articulate what they actually want. Rending control back from groupthink and discovering who you actually are capable of being requires mentally altering these superimposed personas and realizing you are so much more than one or two attributes.

HIJACK YOURSELF

Ask the most profound and wondrous questions possible, then give them thoughtful answers. This practice hijacks the mind, using *The Wonder Effect,* into moving us toward our goals and dreams.

KNOW YOURSELF

What do those questions look like? The specific wording of the questions doesn't necessarily matter, but their structure should focus on how you envision your ideal future. By focusing on a target, it gives space for creativity. Stephen Covey, the author of *The 7 Habits of Highly Effective People*, argues that we should always begin with the end in mind. Rediscovering ourselves is made easier when we structure these profound questions with specific end points and results.

To determine an end, think about time frames that feel commemorating to you. What feels like a future milestone for you? It could be one year, five years, or twenty-five years from now (or any other figure). By that end point, ask yourself what accomplishments or experiences you want to have that you would be proud of. After you consider a thoughtful answer to where you want to be at your chosen milestone, ask yourself *why* you would be proud of those things. Thoughtful answers only.

If that framework doesn't produce a new understanding of your true interests and passions, there is also a self-knowing question, although cliché, that will get the job done. It goes like this: If money wasn't an issue for you, what would you choose to do (either professionally or for fun)? The many answers you may give to that question begin to reveal your true interests. Again, if you feel like this question is too hard to answer, consider priming your answer by searching your shelf. What books, magazines, and items populate your room?

They will likely reveal passions that can lead you to an answer to this question.

Of course, when answering, you have to be thoughtful. Even if you answer, "I would sit around all day and watch TV," it nonetheless reveals an opportunity for direction. Wanting to watch TV all day might suggest an interest in the psychology of relaxation or in the language of cinema. Also, what would you watch? Dramas? The History Channel? These answers reveal something about you and your interests.

The "if money were no issue" question is an important question, but it can sometimes overlook important truths about being a human. For example, a dream to become an astronaut may not reveal a person's total life goals and dreams. In other words, nuanced examination of your dreams, interests, and goals leads to nuanced answers of how you could best accomplish those things.

When exploring these questions, you might be surprised how soon your most authentic passions and interests come to the surface. One could realize they want to work as a gaffer in film and television. Another that they want to run an apple orchard. Yet another that they want to travel to experience new cultures. By asking yourself meaningful questions and responding with thoughtful examination—recorded somewhere, such as in a journal—you will have hijacked your own mind into getting to know your ambitions better, putting them closer within reach.

KNOW YOURSELF

These specific questions might not be the only questions, but they provide a great initial framework to get started. I'll never forget how the lesson of hijacking my own mind was imparted on me by Harvard business professor Marty Marshall. He gave me the advice to buy a notebook and write down the things that interested me most and start learning more about them. I wrote three things: finance, real estate, and manufacturing. At the time, I hardly knew anything about those topics. I had been raised in a family of broadcasters. I penned those three interests somewhat fleetingly because of a belief that I would go into broadcasting like my parents.

Later, when I started my first company and developed television programming, it was so aligned with broadcasting that Professor Marshall's exercise didn't seem relevant. It seemed like I was pigeonholing myself based on my upbringing. As time went on and I continued to transition through several careers naturally and outwardly, which included helping establish a school, I found that I was incrementally pointing back to the ideas in that notebook.

Many years later, I was professionally and intimately involved in all three notebook entries. My primary business was real estate and required me to be in charge of all the complex financial issues involved. On occasion, I needed to manufacture custom items for specific building projects. It is as if, all those years before, I had hijacked my own mind and began a journey to knowing myself. And the same can be true for you. As long as you get to know yourself and put your foot forward in a direction that interests you, your path will likely come full circle to manifest the things you want most.

In the same way your mind can be hijacked by social myths when you are young, you have to hijack your mind as an adult to learn on your own terms. As you journey in that direction, you collect a diverse array of experiences that relate to your multiple interests, quilting a valuable and unique-to-you expertise and perspective.

YOUR LIFE AS A QUILT

After you get to know yourself and seek experiences that interest you, your life quilt starts stitching together naturally. One event will lead to the next. Our experiences don't necessarily need to translate into a career or some specific financial gain. Instead, give yourself permission to discover new patches to your quilt, and continue to get to know yourself. If you are interested in playing the guitar, learn how to play without pressuring yourself to become the next Hendrix. Having learned how to play the guitar may impart a worthwhile lesson you can use in another aspect of your life.

Made up of a set of experiences unique to you, your quilt will be full of diverse patches that add up to valuable and malleable expertise. With each new patch and experience, the mosaic's uniqueness will be on display. One patch will complement the color or pattern of another. You may learn

KNOW YOURSELF

lessons from one life event that you can apply in new contexts you never thought imaginable.

This was something my son experienced for himself. At age eleven, he was very interested in photography. By age thirteen, he applied for and was hired to take pictures at a somewhat prestigious national tennis tournament called the Connecticut Open. Essentially, it was the lead-in tournament to the US Open. So, it was no small accomplishment on his part. When he came home from that gig, he told me that he had learned an important lesson in sports photography. Directly training the camera on the subject would result in a bad photo, he recalled. He said that to get the right shot, you had to anticipate what the athlete was going to do. You had to try to see a little bit into the future based on body movement and then take a photo of the spot where you anticipated the athlete would be.

At that moment, my son believed he had learned a lesson that applied strictly to sports photography. However, as he continued to add experiences to his life's quilt and got old enough to manage his own life, he realized that there is a somewhat universal importance to his lesson of anticipation. Now he is frequently anticipating future trends and working to leverage those insights into opportunities. In my opinion, my son's experience at the Connecticut Open was a patch in his quilt that gave him a different and unique perspective through which he approaches new experiences, and he has the unique ability to anticipate the actions of others.

It's impossible to know how each new experience you have will impact you. But when you approach new experiences because they align with your genuine interests, it's virtually impossible that it won't have a positive impact and lead to beautifully unexpected things. Maybe the impact is joy, a dream career, a hard-earned lesson, more time spent with loved ones, a creative outlet, or any number of other things. That the impact is positive is the important result.

After you discover your interests and internalize the idea that the mere pursuit of those interests will have a positive effect on your future, you also need to be cognizant of *how* you best learn and experience new things. This will help you continue to learn about yourself on your own terms.

YOUR TERMS AND CONDITIONS

You can more easily add patches to your life's quilt if you go about learning and experiencing things in a way that is right for you. More often than not, systems of learning do not serve the individual's needs nor create an environment of success. When you look at school curricula, you will find that they are designed to hit the largest population possible, around 80 percent of the students. So, what happens to the other 20 percent whose background or style doesn't conform to the standard? They are expected to adapt their styles to the single system chosen by a given educational institution.

KNOW YOURSELF

When an individual's learning style is ignored, this creates a profound systemic issue that incorrectly tells them there is something wrong with them, and it inhibits their ability to learn on their own terms. (Many educational institutions are trying to experiment with UDL, or universal design of learning, that does cater to each student's background and style of learning, but this process is in its infancy.)

While I'm using schools as an example, the same principle holds true with all systems that create our perceived identities—the way one might think they are a klutz. To combat this educational inequity, get to know yourself better, and give yourself permission to pursue your interests in a way that speaks to you. Come to know the methods or models by which you feel engaged with your interests.

There are many models that categorize learning processes. Neil Fleming's popular VARK model of learning suggests each individual learns through a specific modality: visual, aural, reading and writing, or kinesthetic. Once you find your style, make sure that you pursue your interests in a way aligned with that style.

Applying this to myself, I am definitely a reading and writing learner, whereas one of my daughters is a visual learner. When we read books, we have very different approaches because of our different learning styles and experiences. When she was in high school, her preference was to read her textbooks on a screen to eliminate the burdensome intimidation of how thick and heavy textbooks are. *Kudos to her*, I thought, *for finding a way to eliminate that sinking feeling of carrying a way-too-heavy textbook around.* I, on the other hand, prefer to read physical books.

You don't have to use Fleming's VARK model to find out how you prefer to experience and learn things, but the point is hopefully taken. Perhaps you prefer to learn everything you can before jumping into experiences. Or perhaps you prefer to learn through experience to eliminate the analysis paralysis that comes from the information dump of studying. Find and use your own system if VARK doesn't speak to you. But you need to discover your own unique style of learning and modify your experiences to best suit your growth style.

When you know yourself and give yourself the space to grow, you begin to adventurously explore things that used to seem impossible. This is what happened with Fred Smith, somebody whose work has affected all of us. The founder of FedEx, Smith's internationally successful company began as a startup that solicited investors.

One day, Smith walked into the offices of my father's employer and pitched his idea. The general reaction to him was, "What? You're going to attempt to compete with the US Post Office? It will never work." Everyone in the room except for Smith was trained to think with a single-minded, limiting, and system-perpetuating perspective. But because Smith decided to approach his interests on his own terms and pursue his passions, he became hugely successful. Next time you get a non-USPS package in the mail, remember that it was once believed such a thing couldn't happen.

During Smith's pitch, the room failed to see Smith's vision because they were comparing his idea to what was already out there. Compared to the USPS, nothing could work as efficiently, the thinking went. However, they all forgot an important lesson about the obstructing nature of comparison.

COMPARING IS (MOSTLY) DESPAIRING

By definition, comparing yourself to others is the opposite of knowing yourself. If you are going to truly know yourself and open up a path toward your interests, you must avoid comparing yourself to others.

Here is where I'll step in to add one big caveat. There are actually two kinds of comparison. The most common one, and the one to be avoided, I call *validation comparison*. The other, much rarer kind that can have a positive impact on us I call *motivational comparison*.

Let's address validation comparisons first. Why is it that folks tend to compare themselves to others? Whether comparing romantic relationships, jobs, vacation habits, looks, or anything else, people evaluate their success or failure relative to the other person. In this way, the comparison is quite similar to Dennis Prager's Missing Tile Syndrome, which he coined in his book *Happiness Is a Serious Problem: A Human*

Nature Repair Manual. According to the theory, by nature, people tend to focus on what they are missing rather than what they have. The analogy of a tile mosaic is used. If you are looking at a beautiful mosaic made up of hundreds of tiles that form a vivid image of some kind, and there is even just one tile missing somewhere within the mosaic, the eye will immediately be drawn to the missing tile. Rather than focus on the beauty of what is in front of us, the eye is compelled to be distracted from the entire mosaic and instead concentrate on the small part that's absent.*

When you compare yourself to others, you only see the few missing tiles in your life's mosaic and not the entire, beautiful image that is present and evident. This diminishes your positivity, gratitude, motivation, and a number of other empowering qualities. Without these, the positive growth from *The Wonder Effect* begins to disappear.

What's worse is *who* people tend to compare themselves to. Most choose glamorous celebrities, social media influencers, or coworkers who just got the promotion. Comparison in any form—desirable external or internal attributes—always leads to a sense of inferiority and a feeling of missing what you have. Validation comparison kills any motivation to know yourself deeply and take action toward your interests in order to remain unique.

---

* Dennis Prager, *Happiness Is a Serious Problem: A Human Nature Repair Manual* (William Morrow, New York), 1988.

KNOW YOURSELF

Some of us are outliers and use validation comparison to compare ourselves to somebody we perceive to be beneath us. In these situations, the results are the same. Those who lift their nose with a sense of superiority feel like they have "made it" and have become the best version of themselves. This mistaken satisfaction thwarts any desire to continue exploring the nuances of their interests and halts any growth in new directions. The stifling effects of validation comparison can't be ignored, and you've got to do your best to stop the comparing habit, turn inward, and get to know yourself.

This all sounds abstract though. How might either version of validation comparison actually occur? Let's explore a concrete but hypothetical example. A community college student who is the best basketball player in their region is on the cusp of earning a scholarship to a major university. If they fall into the trap of validation comparison and decide to compare themselves to Michael Jordan—the best basketball player of all time who very few players can be compared to—they may think, *What is wrong with me? There is no way that I could ever get to that level.* So, they stop honing their skills and fail to earn the scholarship.

Let's go the other way now. This player compares themselves to players from a winless rival school and thinks, *Wow! Compared to them, I am a great player!* Their inflated sense of self prevents them from continuing to improve because they know they can easily beat the so-called competition.

In either direction, the student no longer sees any need to improve how they play basketball. During the process of comparing to validate their feelings of inferiority or superiority, they instill a fixed mindset whose stifled motivation causes them to fall short of receiving scholarship letters from universities. Their dream to play basketball at the next level dies.

Do you recall a time in your life when you used comparison to validate or justify your own lack of growth? Like the student athlete in the above story, it's common to enact the same kind of inhibitive comparisons all the time. *Motivational* comparison is the one exception. Surprisingly, it can encourage action and positive growth. This type of comparison is when you realize that both you and the other person have strengths *and* weaknesses.

What would a motivational comparison look like? The key factor is finding a person you can look at and say, *Wow, they didn't have a special leg up on their journey to their accomplishments. They didn't know the right people to put them on the inside track. They wholly made it themselves.* The lesson they embody is, "If they can do it, I can do it too." For me, an example would be Don Wenner. One couldn't describe his upbringing as an advantage, but now he runs a billion-dollar company, DLP Capital. Like me, Wenner works in real estate. Motivationally, I found it incredibly useful to look up to Wenner as someone I could strive to emulate. Listening to podcasts and reading books, it became clear that Wenner and others were regular people, just folks willing to put in the work to see gains. That realization helped me join their ranks.

When using motivational comparison, you will find that there is nothing that precludes you from the success you see in the other individual. You do not judge the other individual. You recognize their strengths as strengths you can share. You can respond with, "I can do that too!"

When using validation comparison, you compare yourself to find reasons as to why you *can't* or *shouldn't* do things. When trying to validate your own worthiness, you'll always come up short in the end and ignore getting to know yourself. But with the much rarer motivational comparison, you will become curious and look for reasons why you *can* do something. And when you give yourself the opportunity to lead with curiosity and optimism, you increase your potential for the wonder mindset.

WONDER-MINDEDNESS

When you think of close-minded people, what does that mean? Usually, it means they shut down new ideas and are unwilling to ask or entertain questions, let alone pursue the answers. They tend not to be curious. Every answer is a quick and terse no. And they utilize every limitation one could imagine.

Open-mindedness is the exact opposite of all of those things. Open-minded people are willing to take suggestions, consider alternatives, and ask curious questions while pursuing the answers. Being open-minded is an excellent start to crushing false idols and getting to know ourselves, but it is not enough. In order to achieve success, you need to become wonder-minded—a central tenet of *The Wonder Effect*.

Wonder-minded people go beyond the curiosity of open-mindedness by also behaving with optimism and creativity. With curiosity, creativity, and optimism, you create connections between things that may not have obvious connections and, in so doing, you and the world are given the capacity to uncover new things. Being wonder-minded is nothing short of making new discoveries about yourself and the world.

That all sounds fine. But what might wonder-mindedness look like? As a thought experiment, let's say a person has a passion for cameras because of the camera's ability to document reality and capture real-life moments. Being curious and creative, this person takes apart cameras and reads guides on how the internal mechanisms work. Going down that rabbit hole, and learning the science and engineering involved in cameras, could naturally lead them to exploring possible improvements to those mechanisms. Maybe they discover how to install a bigger f-stop range (adjustable size of the aperture) in a smaller package. From there, this person decides they want to manufacture their own camera. This takes them out of the traditional realm of cameras as they begin to learn a new trade of manufacturing—something they never thought would be related to their interests. As they endeavor to manufacture this camera, they come to understand sourcing the raw materials needed and how to manufacture the parts required to make this new, improved camera.

For the close-minded, manufacturing and cameras are two separate things. For the wonder-minded, they could be integrally part of the same passions and interests. With this camera example, though, being wonder-minded sounds a little bit random or haphazard, as if this person accidentally found their way toward manufacturing. But it wasn't an accident. Taking aim at a specific target—an improved camera—naturally led to the manufacturing of this camera. The key here is the action founded on a radical decision based on uncertainty that pulls you toward that future. This would be the "wander" part of the equation, where action and movement are taken after the wondering and imagining of your potential. These actions and beliefs take us in an intentional and serendipitous direction.

KAVANA—OR TARGET PRACTICE?

Kavana is a Hebrew word that primarily means "intention" or "to aim at a specific target." It can also be understood as "focused thought or meditation." When I say *meditation*, I don't mean a quieting of the mind that is common in Eastern forms of meditation. What I'm referring to is closer to discursive meditation, which uses focused and repeated ideas that generate an awareness of yourself. When you choose something to focus on and repeat that idea to yourself, it opens up space to plumb the depths of that topic.

Going back to the camera example, one doesn't always naturally move from being passionate about cameras to manufacturing their own innovative camera. But kavana can help. Once the camera is identified as a passion, create a targeted, open-ended focused thought, such as, *I enjoy and am able to learn everything there is to know about cameras.* When the belief is instilled, the brain and body will start putting in the effort to accomplish this. Manufacturing camera parts and innovating camera design is just one of several possible roads that naturally extends from the gate you've opened.

Over time, these growth-minded affirmations or visualizations can become default beliefs and part of who you are, overriding the fears of your unchosen beliefs. Repeating affirmations enough times, if you believe in the affirmation, will reprogram your beliefs and put energy in actions that lead you toward your dreams and interests.

To be clear, I'm not saying that all you need to do is repeat a phrase like, "I will make significant sums of money" and then the money just starts flowing without effort. But there is an important principle behind using repeated affirmations to override our fears and disempowering beliefs. If you instill beliefs in yourself that help you aim at specific targets, even if they are relatively generic—such as the phrase, "I am capable of overcoming obstacles"—then when obstacles do come, you have made the effort that should click your mind into gear to meet the moment.

KNOW YOURSELF

Internalizing positive affirmations is another form of hijacking your brain to eliminate the stifling fears of social myths and open you up to pursue your interests. To override fears, you have to eliminate or progressively reduce disempowering beliefs from the list of beliefs you carry with you daily.

When I say "carry with you daily," I almost mean that literally. It's important to spend time inventorying the various beliefs you have. When in front of you in a detailed list, you can then reflect on which beliefs are inhibiting and which speak to your ambitious, truer self or the self you want to invent. I say "invent" because relative to your present self, there may be such a huge difference that it would appear as if created out of thin air like an invention.

INVENTORY YOUR BELIEFS

Your beliefs end up dictating what you are capable of accomplishing. It is therefore important that you maintain or create a set of beliefs that represent wonder-minded thinking: open, imaginative, curious, and target-seeking. Doing so will give you conviction and purpose.

By using an inventory of your beliefs, you can identify and eradicate the self-fulfilling prophecies of fixed-mindset beliefs. A negative belief that commonly makes the inventory is, "Bad things always happen to me." As we've discussed, negative beliefs like this create a deeper, unconscious directive to lead you toward things that confirm this belief. If you often see situations in a pessimistic light or believe that bad things always happen to you, it is likely that you are unconsciously making them happen—at least sometimes.

Instead, take an inventory of your beliefs to generate awareness. How do your negative beliefs hold you back? How can you modify your beliefs to deemphasize and eliminate disempowering beliefs? How do your positive beliefs propel you forward? There are many ways to go about inventorying your beliefs, but the simplest way is to be more sensitive to your thoughts. Why? Because your thoughts hold more power than you realize. You are constantly making decisions every day, and when you start becoming more sensitive and aware of the way that you're making those decisions, beneath the surface, you'll start to see the reasoning that you're using, which is essentially somewhat of a belief. For example, you might say that you don't want to try something new because you're not really good at picking up new things. Even though that's not inherently true, it becomes a belief that you have about yourself.

Journal your experiences too. Examine the explanations you give for why you haven't done something or why things are the way they are. This is sometimes easier to do with a trusted friend or partner.

When you don't inventory these beliefs and continue to expect that something is not possible, you spend no energy or effort trying to prove yourself incorrect. The opposite is true when you modify your beliefs to realize that most anything is possible. So why not inventory your beliefs and hold onto any that could be described as growth- or wonder-minded? Odds are that positive change occurs and then builds momentum for more growth.

Recently, scientists have discovered that maintaining growth-minded beliefs provides innumerable benefits to our mental health and capacity for action. Neuroplasticity has shown that one can acquire and utilize a growth mindset at any stage of their life, but children are especially disposed toward this.

What children believe to be true has a large impact on their development. Studies have demonstrated that children with a growth mindset feel more motivation and joy to learn, increased academic achievement, and less depression and anxiety compared to those with a fixed mindset.* Having a growth mindset versus a fixed mindset is something we teach our children, so it is imperative that we help foster growth mindedness. And it is important we socially instill the importance of a growth mindset into the many adults who have succumbed to feeling fixed.

The successes that follow a growth mindset and wonder-mindedness are plentiful. One of my favorites involves the

---

* Jennifer Smith, "Growth Mindset vs. Fixed Mindset: How What You Think Affects What You Achieve," Mindset Health, September 25, 2020, https://www.mindsethealth.com/matter/growth-vs-fixed-mindset.

story of the Wright brothers. They inventoried their beliefs in 1896 and listed something not commonly believed at the time: humans have the capacity for flight. In utilizing their imaginative wonder-mindedness, they operated the first flight of a powered, heavier-than-air aircraft by 1903. In just seven years, they demonstrated to the world that the impossible was actually possible. A belief could become a reality. When you believe it can be done, you will push yourself in the direction of that belief's fulfillment. Inhibiting beliefs block you from your potential to make significant contributions to the world.

The classic example of a limiting belief is time. It's probably the most common thing people will say: "I don't have enough time." I'm here to inform you that this is a bold-faced lie you are telling yourself. If you inventoried that belief and started actually looking at where you are spending your time, you might be surprised at how wrong this common form of fixed-mindedness really is. Adding up the hours of your day, you might realize that you do nothing to pursue your passions during your work commute when you could be listening to an educational podcast or book. You might realize that you spend several hours in the evening on social media or watching YouTube or Netflix. We spend time on so many things that are frivolous and unaligned with our passions that it's just kind of silly when you start comparing the facts against the belief.

KNOW YOURSELF

A fixed mindset is unhealthy and does nothing to power you forward toward your goals. Acknowledge those beliefs and replace them with growth-minded beliefs and actions. For example, as it pertains to transforming the "I don't have enough time" belief, repeat a new affirmation to yourself: "I can reclaim my time." Hijacking your brain, you will start looking for places in your schedule to reclaim. Perhaps you reclaim your mornings, wake up earlier, and accomplish more before the later part of the day brings its fatigue.

What you repeatedly tell yourself is who you become. It reminds me of the central takeaway from Hal Elrod's wonderful book *The Miracle Morning*. One of his arguments is that in order to have a different set of results, you have to become a different person.* When replacing your fixed-mindset beliefs with growth-mindset beliefs, you will be doing just that: replacing your fixed mindset with your new, wonder-minded self that is fully tapped into your true or new nature. Doing so will help you understand your unique capacity. As you become a different person—as you become the person you mindfully choose to be—you will find that you get a different result. Namely, success or fulfillment. As Elrod wrote, "Where you go depends entirely on who you choose to be, from this moment on."†

---

* Hal Elrod, *The Miracle Morning: The Not-So-Obvious Secret Guaranteed to Transform Your Life Before 8 A M*, Hal Elrod Publishers, 2012.

† Elrod, *The Miracle Morning*, 55.

(RE)TRAIN THE ELEPHANT

Knowing yourself again means cutting the rope that trained you to have disempowering beliefs. When cut, you can become an energetic, focused, and adventurous elephant ready to throw the enormous weight of your imagination at your passions and dreams.

Because you are unique and have a different approach than anyone else, your life's quilt will put you on a unique path, manifesting success and the truth that you have a massive amount of untapped capacity. Those patches will stitch your approach to your ambitions in never-before-considered ways, helping you innovate and tap into your imagination and curiosity.

Knowing yourself fully, you can discover and embrace your own ambitions, goals, intentions, and dreams. Once reacquainted with your potential self, a path will open up before you. And as you begin to travel that path, your life's curriculum and your adventures will start to take shape.

CHAPTER 3

LIFE AS A CURRICULUM

Life isn't about finding yourself. Life is about creating yourself.

—GEORGE BERNARD SHAW

I often meet with a group of fellow real estate investors and managers. Within this group, I can safely say that everyone is incredibly successful. They are perfect candidates for motivational comparison. During a recent meeting, I felt a larger-than-normal sense of imposter syndrome. We were discussing how to implement a new management system. While on paper it sounded great, I didn't fully understand how it could be implemented in practice. As people talked, a sinking feeling came over me that I would leave the meeting as the only person out of the loop. And for whatever reason, a part of me didn't want to share my confusion for fear of looking incompetent. But then, the most successful member of the group interrupted the conversation. They didn't understand this proposed system either. Then the dominoes of confession started to fall, and it turned out that everybody was having the same experience. All of these very successful people were struggling with the same thing and, on top of that, were apprehensive about admitting it in front of the group.

By being true to himself first and foremost, this member raised and received answers to excellent questions. The rest of us, it seemed, were willing to kick the can of possible problems down the road. The lessons I learned in that moment were many. First, it turns out that even successful people are afraid of how they are perceived. In the face of that fear, those willing to neutralize it will continue to question and generate more learning and better ideas. In turn, those threads of learning and exploration weave together to form the patches of life's quilt. Using this process, you can ensure a wonder-minded growth outward. It will have a life curriculum either with clear steps to take or with the spontaneous, emerging lessons that can backfill what follows. This is a daily practice, a repetitive and incremental strategy to build out a life curriculum that has been practiced by countless individuals to achieve their dreams.

Let's talk about this "life curriculum" a little bit further. In the context of education, a curriculum is the totality of the student's educational experience as it relates to the planned instructional goals of the instructors and school. But that

LIFE AS A CURRICULUM

traditional definition is not what I am talking about here. The difference is that with a life curriculum, *you* choose the sequence of explorations that educate you. They are not defined for you. Many will be planned and thought out (such as founding a company) or serendipitous (such as being contacted out of the blue for collaborating on a new venture). Regardless, *you* are choosing a subject and going down that rabbit hole.

Weaving these threads together, there is a gap between where you are and where you want to be. You will have some tools that can help you get there, but there are quite a bit of tools you *don't* have, and acquiring them will become a part of your life's curriculum. Understanding what tools to cultivate can sometimes be overt or covert, and it requires exploration. To illustrate, let's say somebody wanted to become a famous magician. What do they have now? Perhaps they've studied how-to books and are already quite good at performing magic. Yet they are not getting any recognition or crowds to enable fame. They will need to explore soft skills such as marketing, charisma, networking, and many others before becoming a headliner. These are no different than the checkpoints, if you will, in academia. In order to get to where you want to go, you have to pass the "test" and keep going.

Being laser-focused on exploring what you need creates a life curriculum that helps you address problems along the way to the goal. To cultivate a curriculum for life, you need to recognize where you are at a given moment, where you want to go, what you have already, and what you need to get you there.

DREAM INTO DOING

Walt Disney made his career by starting something new and letting the problems that presented themselves act as a guide for his life curriculum. By the time of his death, he had created Mickey Mouse, the most famous character in entertainment history, a successful film studio, a theme park enterprise (that would soon turn into an entertainment empire), and he even had plans to redesign the modern American city. From short films, to feature films, to theme parks, to cities, his journey displayed quite a progression of success.

During each step of the process, it is fair to say that he was no expert in the particular fields where he excelled. Disney's success consisted of a curriculum of *starting* down a path and finding ways to become an expert along the way. When he opened his first, modest animation studio, he did so with a partner, Ub Iwerks. While Disney had some ability to draw, it was Iwerks who was the animation guru, designing Mickey Mouse from Walt's imagination and instructions.

After a while, Walt became interested in theme parks, a mostly unproven venture at that time. Again, he was no engineer, architect, or area planner. What should the design philosophy be? What would the ultimate storytelling theme park look like? He started with these kinds of questions. This then led him to seek the right people and, after work and effort, Disneyland eventually became the success we know it to be.

Walt Disney had a growth mindset. Utilizing kavana, he aimed at specific targets that gave him the drive and purpose to accomplish something greater than himself. By putting in the effort—to start and not stop—he utilized a life curriculum that emphasized a fresh perspective and energetic determination. This, in turn, positively impacted the experts he gathered to help him achieve his dreams.

I'm not saying that Disney or Disneyland *must* be appreciated by everybody, but I am emphasizing the important role that simply starting had for Disney's objective successes. When we deconstruct the methods by which Disney cultivated success, we see that it was in the starting and the learning along the way.

Disney might seem like an outlier because his successes were outsized, but so, too, were his failures. He lost the rights to his first character, Oswald the Lucky Rabbit. He lost money on almost every movie he made until *Cinderella*. Disney was able to overcome his failures because he tried to learn from them and continued to start new ventures. In success or failure, he would question the method and continue asking new questions to generate different results.

START AT THE START

Your life's curriculum is a framework by which you approach your passions with intentionality, curiosity, and a desire to constantly grow. When you push yourself in the direction of your passions, you inevitably ask yourself what it will take to innovate and succeed. Answering those questions will help you develop your curriculum.

Although every person's curriculum will be unique to their total experiences, there are basic ways in which you can build out its details. There are question frameworks, such as Don Wenner's, that you can use for this purpose. For my part, I believe you should ask yourself three questions frequently:

- What are the things you want to continue doing?

- What are the things you want to stop doing?

- What are the things you need to start doing?

By thoughtfully answering these questions in detail, you will be able to realign your habits and choose the tools that end up carving you, that shape you, and that determine your capacity.

Because you are learning as you go, the syllabus of your curriculum gets backfilled, in a way. If you start with goals, passions, and interests, your syllabus begins to fill up with things to explore. That exploration then creates new skills or knowledge, and you are on the path to success through that curriculum. And then it gets constantly adjusted as you experiment. It sounds counterintuitive to put the pieces together as you go, but that is a successful formula. Experiment to see what works and what doesn't.

Once you start, you learn as much basic information as you can and build from there, perhaps starting by reading *The Dummies Guide to* . . . whatever you're pursuing. Or find instructional videos from YouTube or elsewhere. Quickly, after you take action, you will realize that you don't know everything you need to succeed. As soon as that aha moment arrives, your experience now shows you the gaps that you need to fill by learning. As you invest your life and energy into this project, it starts taking shape naturally. You budget for it, write out the ideas, create data points, prove or disprove your hypothesis, and so on.

CHOOSE THE TOOLS THAT CARVE YOU

As much as it is true that we are in control of ourselves, there are external factors that often shape who we are. In many cases, though, we can change the external tools that carve or shape us. You have limited control of your environment but can harness that environment to improve the probability of success. There are four general external factors that create who you are:

- your society (local groups, colleagues, and people you choose to be around)

- your household (immediate community, like family and friends)

- your genes (aptitude, height, gender—predetermined)

- your education habits (schools you attend, how you study)

While you can't change your genes (yet), you can control the other three factors to some degree. The society you belong to, your household, and your education habits are all things that you can alter at any given moment to develop new, positive habits.

There's a popular quote often attributed to poet John Dryden: "We make our habits and then our habits make us." So, *make* your habits. You have control over your society, household, and education habits. Whether you consciously know it or not, you choose them constantly. You choose who you spend time with. You choose who to include in your family once you are older and out of the house. And you choose how to educate yourself. Without knowing it, you have a set of habits that are, as Dryden would phrase it, "making" you. Tailor them to have a positive impact on your life's curriculum.

Among the external factors that shape you, mentor relationships are among the most important. These carefully cultivated experts are people who you put your trust in. They guide you as you develop and implement a curriculum in pursuit of your interests.

SEEK MENTORSHIP

A mentor (the type I recommend) has seen or is in closer proximity to the destination you seek, and can give "directions" how to navigate there based on your present location.

Therefore, choosing a mentor should be done with care and caution. People love to help and give advice—or, more often, their opinions—but there are several guidelines to follow when curating those people who will have the most impact on your goals. Author Darren Hardy argues that if your vision is bigger than the people you are getting advice from, they're not the right people to get that advice from. Conversely, if you would want to trade places with the person, you're getting advice from, you are talking to the right person.

Sometimes your options for mentors appear narrow. If that's the case, you need to get creative. Tony Robbins and Peter Diamandis were inventive in seeking mentors when they founded an insurance company aimed at giving patients precision medical analyses. In short, they wanted to provide insurance based on *preventing* illness rather than *treating* illness. Neither person had expertise in medical insurance, so they spoke to the appropriate health providers, insurance companies, and other mentors who were able to help them successfully launch their company.

What curriculum prompted both men to believe that the healthcare insurance industry needed innovation? Peter Diamandis, when interviewed by James Altucher about the book Diamandis coauthored with Tony Robbins, *Life Force*, revealed that the half-life of knowledge doctors learn during their time in medical school is, at most, two years.* Twenty-four months is all it takes before the bulk of information that doctors receive during their nearly decade-long training is no longer relevant. That's a scary thought, and one that suggests the healthcare industry needed to be innovated.

Doctors, obviously, are trained to treat patients. They don't operate in a system that prevents their need to treat patients. A carpenter who works with wood only sees nails for solutions. Diamandis and Robbins used a life curriculum and pursued mentors to develop alternative solutions in healthcare. They maintained an open mind, explored, and are constantly seeking ways to eliminate the traditional and potentially dangerous forms of healthcare insurance. They found people at the highest levels and at the forefront of their field in the development of their company.

---

* James Altucher, "822—Tony Robbins and Peter Diamandis: How New Breakthroughs in Precision Medicine Can Transform the Quality of Your Life," February 17, 2022, in *Simplecast*, podcast, MP3 audio, 1:03:18, https://jas.simplecast.com/episodes/822-tony-robbins-peter-diamandis-I6nqJ1Dr.

LIFE AS A CURRICULUM

When you want to pursue an interest, a career, a hobby, a passion, or anything of the sort, you should start reaching out to the people necessary to make that exploration meaningful. The best mentors for your pursuits will become clearer as you start pulling on that thread of interest or passion.

Even for the most unusual or "weirdest" pursuits, the mentors are clear. Take, for example, writer, actor, and comedian Fred Armisen. In interviews, stand-up specials, and elsewhere, Armisen has discussed the mentoring hand director John Waters had on his success. The story goes that, while still in high school, Armisen submitted a homework assignment he intended to be humorous. Instead, it landed him in the school psychiatrist's office. Confused by the discouragement, he wrote to his idol, John Waters, whom he admired and emulated in his comedic stylings. Armisen explained to Waters that the incident shook his confidence in his own artistic abilities. Surprisingly, Waters replied to his fan. In the return letter of encouragement, Waters told Armisen that he was on the right path and should continue embracing the unique weirdness of his comedy. Years later, that path took Armisen to *Saturday Night Live*. After that, he cocreated unique and internationally famous shows like *Documentary Now!* and *Portlandia*.

Like Armisen did with Waters, you need to reach out to mentors not because they give you a golden ticket, but because it creates connection and direction. Mentors hardly ever lead you to the gold at the end of the rainbow. But they will point you toward a direction in which you will have a greater degree of confidence moving forward. From there, you will be more empowered to emotionally or intellectually dust yourself off as you stumble along the way.

For Armisen, Waters acted as an influencing mentor, or somebody who affected the development or character of a person. Influencing mentors may not give you explicit advice on technical or legal things, but they have an important emotional and generative effect on you. They do this by lending credence to your belief in yourself by having the ability to connect with them. They're humanized, which bridges the possibility of rising to their level. They thus gain more credibility in your mind and heart. And the guidance that they provide implicitly is a statement that the pursuit is possible.

In addition to influencing mentors, there are at least two other types: advisors and connectors. Advisor mentors will help you learn new information about specific matters. If you are an aspiring artist, an advisor mentor might show you which brushes are most effective for certain painting techniques. If you are learning how to be an investor in real estate, an advisor mentor might teach you due diligence. Going back to the example of Peter Diamandis and Tony Robbins, they worked strictly with advisor mentors while creating their precision-medicine insurance company.

After influencers and advisors come the connector mentors. These go-betweens are folks who help you connect with the right advisor mentors. You'd be surprised at how wide of a net you can cast when you reach out to your connections. For example, at the time of writing, I am currently working on an out-of-state deal to buy property. Because each state has their own nuanced laws, I contacted a connector mentor who lives in the state in question. Because I trust him and have kept up a regular relationship with him, I asked him to recommend a real estate lawyer who could answer some of my questions. To my surprise, he happened to be good friends with one of the most prestigious lawyers in the state and was happy to give me a wonderful and flattering introduction.

When you foster these positive relationships with mentors, there are few things as exciting as the real-time growth they provide. Mentors who have achieved substantial success in their respective fields have a clear perspective on the steps required. Because their vision can see beyond yours at the moment, they can guide you through any fog obstructing your vision.

It's important to add that not all mentors need to be people you directly communicate with frequently. Nor do they need to be currently living. No, that wasn't a typo. Some of the most potent mentors can be those who have passed on, but you are significantly influenced by the impact they left on the world. Maybe you have never met them, like a bestselling author or researcher from decades ago who lives on through their books and teachings. Mentors could also be podcast hosts or coaches. Immerse yourself in a mentor's ideas from afar if their work is available to you.

Musical artists are a great example of people who harness mentors from afar. The pop-punk band Green Day was known to listen to albums by The Kinks during their recording sessions in order to absorb some of the qualities they believed represented excellent pop-punk music. Or consider filmmaker Orson Welles, director of what is widely considered to be the greatest film ever made, *Citizen Kane*. While making *Citizen Kane*, he reportedly watched John Ford's *Stagecoach* thirty-nine times during production to influence his artistic decisions. Mentors who guide us need not be face-to-face.

But when you are interacting with them, frequent and open communication is the best way to foster a positive relationship. It could be an email, an email blast to multiple people, a text, a social media post, a social media direct message, a phone call, or writing a letter. At conferences or meetups, communication could even be through informal luncheons. Emphasize that you are asking for advice and direction so the people you reach out to know how to help you.

In the process of fostering a relationship with them, make sure that you ask permission to continue to ask for advice and guidance from them, including if you can consistently follow up with them. You want the relationship to be mutual, meaningful, and collaborative. You are not using them; the two of you are working together toward common goals because you are like-minded. As you collaborate with this person, you don't necessarily need to ask, "Will you be my mentor?" Instead, explain that there are things you are pursuing that may be outside your realm of expertise and you'd appreciate their perspective. While discussing those issues, ask if it would be okay to come to them with specific questions.

When obstacles arise, mentors may provide the experience and insight that help you overcome the hurdle. That obstacles *will* come up, reveals another critical component to your life's curriculum. You don't need to be a genius to accomplish great things. You simply need to put in the time, effort, and energy.

TIME, EFFORT, AND ENERGY

Avoid thinking that you need to be a genius to grow into new areas of possibility. There are many ways to behave smartly. In fact, intelligence is so broad and dynamic that many experts offer varying theories on its functions. We've heard about the IQ (intelligence quotient), but today there is a push to understand the EQ (emotional intelligence quotient). Or if you prefer, "book smarts" and "street smarts." The 1983 book *Frames of Mind*, authored by Professor Howard Gardner of Harvard University, famously categorized eight types of intelligence:

- **Spatial intelligence:** shows keen visual and spatial judgment

- **Bodily-kinesthetic intelligence:** links physical movement and motor control

- **Musical intelligence:** displays rhythmic and musical talent

- **Linguistic intelligence:** demonstrates a control of words, language, and writing

- **Logical-mathematical intelligence:** analyzes problems and mathematical operations

- **Interpersonal intelligence:** understands and reacts to others

- **Intrapersonal intelligence:** displays introspection and reflection

- **Naturalistic intelligence:** sees patterns in nature*

Professor Gardner's model, and many others like it, demonstrate that there is no single way to be brilliant. Regardless of how you understand intelligence, the variety of intelligence

---

* Kumar Mehta, "A Harvard Psychologist Says Humans Have 8 Types of Intelligence. Which Ones Do You Score Highest In?," Make It, *CNBC*, March 10, 2021, https://www.cnbc.com/2021/03/10/harvard-psychologist-types-of-intelligence-where-do-you-score-highest-in.html.

LIFE AS A CURRICULUM

types tells us that genius is not a prerequisite for intelligence. One need not be a genius to cultivate and wield a strong intelligence on their way to personal growth and success.

And these intelligences are not inherent; they can be developed. Somebody can, let's say, develop the interpersonal intelligence necessary to build an amazing team. When you develop intelligence in a certain area, that sharpens specific skills. Maybe you are amazing at systems, or you are especially good at writing app software. Or, perhaps, you have an intuitive understanding of personal dynamics. These skills are an offshoot of intelligence and effort.

In order to gain intelligence, you need to put in the time, effort, and energy to acquire it and then, most importantly, *apply it*. The application of intelligence at its finest results in experience and wisdom. There's the old adage that differentiates intelligence and wisdom. It states that intelligence is knowing that a tomato is a fruit, and wisdom is knowing not to put a tomato in a fruit salad. In other words, intelligence is knowing and understanding concepts and information; whereas wisdom puts that knowledge into its full context to create action. Wisdom creates the foresight that fosters success.

It's actually rare for geniuses to implement good ideas because they are too caught up in their intelligence to have the wisdom to bring them into actuality. So rather than expect yourself to achieve genius status *before* you find success, expect that it will take the blood, sweat, and tears of time, effort, and energy for you to acquire intelligence and wisely bring it into this world. Read, talk to others, and learn. Get the information for yourself. Then be willing to experiment and implement.

Notice that you need to pair time, effort, and energy with *The Wonder Effect*. Although it sounds like a contradiction to both focus time and energy *while* simply wondering what is possible, that is precisely what you need to do. Without that combination, you can't pursue growth-minded actions that are aligned with your interests.

Also, don't overlook the amount of effort you need to put forth. Dr. Angela Duckworth sums up this truth perfectly: "Without *effort*, your talent is nothing more than your unmet potential. Without *effort*, your skill is nothing more than what you could have done but didn't. With *effort*, talent becomes skill and, at the very same time, *effort* makes skill productive."*

And while all three elements—time, effort, and energy—are vital to your life's curriculum, I'd like to draw a special emphasis on time. Success doesn't happen overnight. In fact, as we'll talk about in later chapters, so-called failures are more frequent than successes. Things take longer than you think. After writing a letter to John Waters, Fred Armisen didn't become a famous entertainer overnight. After sparking

---

* Angela Duckworth, *Grit: The Power of Passion and Perseverance* (New York: Scribner, 2016), 51.

the idea for precision medicine, Peter Diamandis and Tony Robbins didn't start a company and then release a book about it the next day. Don't get discouraged when obstacles come your way. Those obstacles are helping you get where you need to go.

Once you start to build some momentum, it's best not to stop. It's very difficult to get going again without immense amounts of discipline and motivation. A close friend of mine who is now eighty-seven decided to never stop pursuing a curriculum of goals. He made golf his focus upon retirement at age sixty-five. Is he going to become the next Tiger Woods or change the world of golf? Unlikely. Does that mean he's not a successful golfer? No! Because he has spent the last two decades putting in the effort and energy to improve, he has seen consistent improvement in his game, which helps him sustain drive, no pun intended, and purpose in his retired life rather than dwindle away from stasis. That is a success manufactured from following a life curriculum, and it shows the importance of never quitting. One way to maintain our curriculum with a sense of purpose is through continued effort and energy to set, maintain, and reevaluate goals.

SET GOALS

There are many methods to help you set and envision goals for yourself. Some are cliché, and some are unique. A popular one is a system called SMART goals created by George Doran, Arthur Miller, and James Cunningham.* SMART—an acronym that stands for specific, measurable, attainable, relevant, and time-based—is a system that hones your ambitions and interests into achievable goals. As you generate goals, you need to make sure they embody each part of the acronym. When a goal meets all five criteria, fulfilling a goal is much more manageable. For example, "My goal is to have a beautiful backyard" is abstract, nondescript, and sets no clear intention. If somebody has a backyard that is several acres, it might not even be achievable in a short amount of time. However, if we tweak it to be a SMART goal, it might read, "My goal is to build two garden beds in my spare time over the next month to beautify my backyard." With this revision, we have created a goal that is specific (garden beds), measurable (two of them), attainable (minimal labor commitment), relevant (it will beautify the backyard), and time-based (one-month window). By virtue of having this SMART goal, we will be more likely to put in the time, effort, and energy to build the garden beds because we have given ourselves a precise curriculum to follow.

Whether or not you use SMART goals or another system entirely, success depends upon creating separate goals for

---

* George T. Doran, "There's a S.M.A.R.T. Way to Write Management's Goals and Objectives," *Management Review* 70, no. 11 (November 1981): 34–35, https://community.mis.temple.edu/mis0855002fall2015/files/2015/10/S.M.A.R.T-Way-Management-Review.pdf.

different periods of time. When you break things up incrementally, goals are more digestible and achievable. I like to have daily, bimonthly, quarterly, yearly, and three-year goals. With this system, I find that working backward from the three-year goals helps me back into the other goals, like falling dominoes. Once the three-year goal is set, I know what I need to accomplish each quarter leading up to that. To accomplish those quarterly goals, I know what I need to accomplish bimonthly. And so on down the line until my daily goals become clear. If the purpose of the life curriculum is to close the gap between where you are and where you want to go, the goals are components within that life curriculum.

Strategies for writing achievable goals and staying incrementally consistent are all well and good, but you may be thinking, *How do I come up with the goals or ideas for them in the first place?* Influenced by James Altucher, a strategy I use is called *idea coupling*. Idea coupling takes seemingly disparate ideas—interests from your life's quilt—that join to create a third, new idea. By mixing vastly different ideas from your life quilt, new ideas that stem from idea coupling will be unique to you. Thinking back to my early work in television programming, it was idea coupling that sparked my combining a live auction and television. Auctions and TV were two separate things I wanted to combine. This innovative idea was successful for quite some time. When those wonderful, innovative ideas emerge, they can be translated into SMART goals.

While the idea-coupling strategy can lead to grand goals, what about naming the smaller goals? That is when your personal research needs to kick in. Identify the skills necessary to achieve what you want. Then, make new goals to attain these skills you've identified through the paths you've researched. As you put yourself in that world, you can get a better understanding of what else you need to do to accomplish the grand idea.

I'll give you an example of moving from macro to micro goals. Once, I gave myself the three-year macro goal to hit a specific amount of real estate income. From that larger goal, I researched and discovered that hitting that macro goal meant acquiring twenty units of a specific kind of real estate, which became another goal. From there, I networked with investors to find out how big my pool of professional relationships needed to be to solicit the number of deals I needed. That became a new goal. Knowing that eventually I would have to sign deals, "learn how to properly conduct real estate investment deals" became yet another goal. Working backward from my macro goal helped me establish the micro goals. Once that ball started rolling, the smaller goals naturally presented themselves.

Smaller goals are so abundant that you should plan to accomplish more than you think you will need. I don't want to be a downer, but it is a fact that there will be goals you do not achieve. And that is okay. Hall of Fame baseball players are only successful at hitting a baseball 30 percent of the

LIFE AS A CURRICULUM

time. In other words, they fail 70 percent of the time and are still heralded as the best to ever play. In the face of failure, your goals should send you in a direction of exploration and growth that can lead to new goals.

BEFORE YOU EXPLORE

Even for the goals you do not achieve, you need to understand the benefits that come with setting goals and giving them time, energy, and effort. Manage your miscues by realizing that goals will stretch you. By their very nature, goals provide space to grow and explore. They bring new things that better ourselves. The skills you pick up when failing will be useful for accomplishing future goals.

When you build out your life's curriculum in this fashion, your ongoing experiences and increasing awareness will give you a growth mindset. In other words, you will be ready to explore all of your interests on your own terms. Even when the dissatisfaction of a missed opportunity sets in, that's when it's time to self-reflect and self-regulate. For example, people sometimes catastrophize. When things are not going in the direction they want, their negative imagination may take over, seeing all the ways this is going to be a complete train wreck. That is a protection mechanism, but you shouldn't entirely shut it down, so self-regulating in this context would mean slowing down that process and not letting it completely take over your thoughts and consequently your feelings. You have to examine the scenario and consider it probabilistically, because often the worst case is extremely unlikely. Even if the worst does happen, you can take the time to also consider what steps you would/could take to mitigate that. Remember, dissatisfaction is actually a good thing and fosters our sense of exploration, as you will come to find out.

CHAPTER 4

EXPLORE ON YOUR OWN

Have the faith to follow a new tomorrow.

—BLESSING OFFER

A fable authored by Professor Amos Dolbear in 1898 made the case for individuals pursuing their own interests and strengths instead of conforming. The *Boston Herald* reprinted a version that read, in part, like this:

> One time the animals had a school. The curriculum consisted of running, climbing, flying, and swimming, and all the animals took all the subjects. The Duck was good in swimming—better, in fact, than his instructor—and he made passing grades in flying, but he was particularly hopeless in running. Because he was low in this subject, he was made to stay after school and drop his swimming class in order to practice running.

He kept this up until he was only average in swimming, but average was passing so nobody worried about that except the Duck. The Eagle was considered a problem pupil and was disciplined severely. He beat all others to the top of the tree in the climbing class, but he always used his own way of getting there. The Rabbit started at the top of the class in running, but he had a nervous breakdown and had to drop out of school on account of so much make-up work in swimming.*

As the fable continues, more animals are introduced, and each have specific-to-them interests and strengths. For this Duck, Eagle, and Rabbit, each animal's abilities are limited by the school's broad approach to train each animal in the same basic skills. But to judge a duck's skills based on its ability to run is asinine. To punish an eagle for flying to the top of a tree instead of climbing is, again, ludicrous. In order to explore their true calling, these animals would need to use the skills unique to them to achieve in their own way and explore their interests on their own terms. Thankfully, you have already learned some crucial steps about questioning the underlying assumptions of social myths. You are now equipped to begin building your life's curriculum and explore

---

* Bill Cunningham, "This and That in Bill's Book," *Boston Herald*, May 4, 1946.

outside of your perceived confines, moving in the direction of your aspirations.

ADVENTUROUS EXPLORATION

You may have been led to believe that almost everything has already been done or discovered. That's why nearly any new discovery is deemed lucky, like finding a gold bar in your backyard. Let's think this through for a moment, because I disagree. There is always room for another breakthrough. One of the more famous examples of a so-called lucky discovery is the history-altering discovery of penicillin—the world's first antibacterial drug—by Scottish physicist Dr. Alexander Fleming. Conducting experiments on bacteria for reasons not related to treating illness, Dr. Fleming noticed one petri dish was contaminated with mold. In that moldy dish, strangely, he noticed that the bacteria seemed to actively avoid the mold. Quickly, he tested the mold further and found that it was an antibacterial substance capable of curing many bacteria-based illnesses.* Since Dr. Fleming's discovery, some estimate that penicillin has saved hundreds of millions of lives. Seems pretty lucky, right? It wasn't.

---

* Robert Gaynes, "The Discovery of Penicillin—New Insights After More than 75 Years of Clinical Use." *Emerging Infectious Disease.* 2017 May;23(5):849–853. doi: 10.3201/eid2305.161556. PMCID: PMC5403050.

Dr. Fleming discovering an antibacterial drug in a bacteria lab is perfectly logical. Where else would a major discovery about bacteria occur than in a bacteria lab? Rather than pure luck, Dr. Fleming cultivated a professional life that was designed to experiment and make discoveries surrounding bacteria. On the other hand, if Dr. Fleming was a poet, accidentally tripped over a moldy petri dish on the way to the pub one day, randomly decided to turn it into a medication in hopes it would work, and then the drug became wildly successful, *that* would be an example of true luck. With this in mind, you can see that the modern usage of the word *luck* means something specific that does not represent its original definition. If luck means putting yourself in the right place at the right time, then yes, Dr. Fleming was lucky. If luck means a series of random and chaotic events that worked out well, then Dr. Fleming was not lucky. To explore our own interests successfully, you need to create your own luck using the "put yourself in the right place at the right time" version of the word.

Sahil Bloom, creator and contributor to *The Curiosity Chronicle*, has talked about the importance of cultivating luck rather than letting it find you. For Bloom, luck is not a series of circumstances that we have no control over. He presented a thought experiment to demonstrate this. If a hypothetical software engineer had a choice between a great job opportunity in Kansas or a good job opportunity in Silicon Valley, which would they choose? In choosing the good-not-great option in tech-heavy Silicon Valley, the worker would surround themselves with more opportunities for more success going forward. They'd be in the right places at the right time. In Kansas, there is little-to-no tech industry. By choosing the superficially worse option with greater chance for long-term success, this software engineer has cultivated their own luck.*

Going back to the four tools that carve us—household, society, genes, and education—we can cultivate our own luck by changing key factors. By experimenting and exploring new inputs that align with our interests, such as traveling to new places, surrounding ourselves with different people, and learning through new experiences, there is a strong chance that the proverbial "lucky situation" will find us.

To explore one's interests effectively, you need to cultivate situations that give you a higher chance at success. If you reread the previous sentence one more time, it seems perfectly obvious. But it can be difficult to cultivate luck because the results from our efforts tend to bring more dissatisfaction than satisfaction. Experiments often fail to yield the desired results. Over time, that can be dissatisfying. Although identified as a negative emotion, dissatisfaction can actually be a good thing.

---

* Sahil Bloom, "How to Get Lucky," March 9, 2022, in *The Curiosity Chronicle*, podcast, MP3 audio, 12:26, https://sahilbloom.substack.com/p/how-to-get-lucky#details.

HOW SATISFYING DISSATISFACTION CAN BE

You read that correctly. Dissatisfaction is a good thing because it can act as a stimulator. Conversely, and perhaps just as surprisingly, satisfaction can be dangerous. Dissatisfaction is the tension between where you are and where you want to be. Say you wanted to be an influential attorney affecting real and positive change in the policies that govern the hundreds of millions of people in our society, but at this point in time you are a grocery store clerk making a positive impact on your local community (a smaller area of positive change). Because there is a tension or a discrepancy between where you want to be and where you are, presumably your life as a store clerk would generate dissatisfaction.

Obviously, this attorney-versus-clerk example has an extreme gulf between this person's present and ideal future. For many, this tension may be a lot more nuanced or smaller. Maybe you were aiming for a 10 percent raise but only received 9 percent, creating a tension that led to dissatisfaction. The point is that when the tension of the dissatisfaction can be named, it should spur you to continue to take action in the direction of your aspirations: "I am still one percent shy of my desired raise. I will work hard and negotiate the rest of my desired raise by the end of the month."

In this 10-percent-raise example, the margin of tension is very thin. However, if healthy doses of dissatisfaction create motivation for continued exploration, it is in your best interests to aim high enough that you are likely to fall just short of your goals and dreams. That way, there will always be a motivational tension driving you toward something unaccomplished. You may think it strange to plan on being unsatisfied when major aspirations are attained, but with success comes different, newer, and exciting possibilities. When you are only partially successful, having remaining goals maintains that sense of tension and forward motion.

Dissatisfaction and its motivational tension drop from the equation entirely when goals are so vague and unprocessed through the self, they can become either too difficult or too easy to accomplish. In these situations, easy or difficult goals can't create new goals.

If you were to accomplish a way-too-easy goal, this would theoretically generate satisfaction. But that rarely happens. When accomplished goals don't lead to new goals, a lack of purpose and emptiness sets in that kills drive. When the eighteen-year-old Olympian wins the gold medal they've been training their entire life for, where do they go from there? What could possibly be higher or the next goal? A disproportionate amount of Olympic athletes experience emotional health issues after their prestigious wins because they have very little left to accomplish beyond Olympic competition.*

---

* John Florio and Ouisie Shapiro, "The Dark Side of Going for Gold," *The Atlantic*, August 18, 2016, https://www.theatlantic.com/health/archive/2016/08/post-olympic-depression/496244/.

Not having continual, long-range goals is one problem. Another is when your goals are too demanding or poorly defined—for example, the goal of becoming wealthy. The receding horizon of what that goal actually means to your unique self will stifle motivation to act toward that goal. You will not feel a motivating dissatisfaction related to coming up just short of specific goals. Instead, the ill-defined goal will be easily susceptible to limiting beliefs that stifle action. "I'm just *this* or *that*. I don't have what it takes to become wealthy." Whatever "wealthy" means to this person with an ill-defined goal, we will never know.

On the face of it, encouraging you to be dissatisfied sounds like I'm advocating for you to be depressed and negative. That's not the case. I believe one can be happy with what they have in the present but simultaneously dissatisfied with unrealized potential. It's not that you should sit around being upset that you haven't accomplished your goals. You shouldn't let your dissatisfaction bleed into other areas of your life, such as scorning your family and friends. Quite the opposite! You should appreciate them. In addition to living with gratitude, motivate yourself with a healthy, tension-filled dissatisfaction that is based upon the fact that you are here for a reason. If you have unrealized potential, it is an indication that there is a purpose and a contribution that you have yet to bring to fruition and completion.

Cultivate the tension between what you want to do, where you want to go, who you want to be, and where you

EXPLORE ON YOUR OWN

are presently by setting goals and choosing the tools that carve you. This is an excellent way to explore your interests. These methods create the curiosity and tension needed to put yourself in the right place at the right time. Doing so helps you perpetually increase your influence and impact, opening up possibilities than you may have initially thought impossible. Over time, you will be positively affecting others and instilling your own life with a growing sense of purpose.

You will find that your purpose may change throughout your life. This occurs because you can't immediately know the implications of all your experiences. If I decided to explore learning the guitar, that might strengthen parts of my mind that make me better at math, which in turn may help me in other areas. The benefits from learning a new skill, such as playing the guitar, will be different for everybody. The point is that there is an element of mystery and serendipity to your growth when it has a constant tension that helps drive you forward. Your branching paths may be divergent but will still magnetically pull you back toward your major interests.

We should always be open to things working out in ways we might not have assumed to be the right way (the mystery in action). As much as you want to plan, you don't want to be so focused that you lose sight of opportunities and growth along the way. Take this anecdotal story, for example:

A man deeply rooted in his faith experiences a shipwreck, ending up stranded on a desert island. When a fishing boat approaches the next day offering rescue, he declines, stating his trust in God's deliverance. A few days later, a cruise ship spots him and dispatches a life raft, which he also refuses, citing his unwavering faith in God's intervention. Finally, a helicopter lands, sent by a wealthy explorer who spotted him. Despite his deteriorating condition, he persists in rejecting aid, clinging to his belief in divine rescue. Tragically, he succumbs to his circumstances, prompting a confrontation with God in the afterlife. In response to his question of why he wasn't saved, God highlights the various forms of assistance sent to him. Even if we're secure in our faith, I think that some of us have a way of viewing *how* God will help us. We might be praying for a miracle, but I suspect that we have visions of *how* that miracle will play out. This can be dangerous, in that our eyes can be closed to the way that God *wants* to help us.

Remember that your successes daisy chain off of one another in the process of exploration. So begin exploring if you haven't begun already. Whatever has stifled your growth must be dealt with as you go toward a future in the direction of your ambitions.

FUTURE MEMORIES

As you pursue your future, keep in mind one simple but powerful truth: whether you've been successful or not, your past results have no bearing on your future results. Generally, the

EXPLORE ON YOUR OWN

past and future have one thing in common: neither one exists. The past was what was, but no longer is. The future hasn't been and can't be known. You may be thinking, *You told me to learn from my experiences, which are in the past.*

I will address that, but for now, let's acknowledge that there is only the present. And in the present, all the decisions that you make are real. These decisions will lead toward future targets. If you have a fixed mindset, your choices will keep your present fixed. If you have a growth mindset, your choices will help you grow. If your past choices have kept you fixed or growing, it doesn't matter. Whoever you were in the past is no longer relevant; it has no bearing because the present is only what matters. Right at this moment, you still have the opportunity to generate a growth or wonder mindset.

If you start making different decisions in the present, it won't matter what happened in the past; your future will be different. How do we know this is true? I think the election of Barack Obama illustrates the point beautifully.

If we were to wrongly argue that history could accurately predict the future instead of the present, then statistically there would have been no chance of Barack Obama becoming president. Until him, all presidents had been White, forecasting the future possibility of a Black president at zero percent. Yet, he became president because he used his present to change the future. When he was inaugurated, everything that happened in the past—in terms of the until-then qualities that defined a president—became irrelevant as President Obama rewrote those possibilities.

Whatever is in the past is in the past. It is, more or less, irrelevant. Past success (or lack thereof) is no guarantee of your future. However, if you've had success in the past, a benefit it offers is making the possibility of success less imaginary and more tactile. For those still waiting to achieve, you will require a strong discipline and imagination because the belief of possibility needs to be integrated into you. Those with past success have already had that belief integrated. With either option—exploring on your own terms with or without previous success—your future is not determined by your past.

Furthermore, don't use past successes to become satisfied in the present. Because the future is not fully guaranteed, it's important not to rest on your laurels or let your guard down by a string of successes thinking that your failure is unlikely. You always need to be exploring anew with fresh curiosities and interests to maximize your growth potential and capacity for achievement and progress.

The decisions, actions, behaviors, and habits in the present end up creating your future self. One way to increase the chances of creating a future you want rests in a concept called *future memories*. Our discussion of future memories, in many respects, will be a continuation of lessons you learned when getting to know yourself again. How do future memories work? It echoes John Dryden's sentiment: "We

EXPLORE ON YOUR OWN

first make our habits and then our habits make us." Except I want to add beliefs to that formula. Because you hold beliefs about who you are, as you grow into your future, those beliefs end up making you who you actually end up becoming.

As with most things, future memories can be positive or negative. Recall our previous discussions pertaining to projected roles in a family unit. For the person who thinks of themselves as the black sheep, that person will likely seek out behaviors in the present that sustains their status as the black sheep going forward. When a sense of victimhood dominates the way you think about your identity, it creates future memories of victimhood, and you will most likely envision—consciously or unconsciously—ways to perpetuate that identity and status.

If you want to break free from inhibiting future memories and adopt successful future memories, you need to choose the identity you want, tell yourself that you are and want to be *that* identity, and program yourself to cultivate that particular future self. If you want to be the kind and empathetic one in the family, then close your eyes, imagine, and visualize what you would be like, look like, feel like, and sound like. Then decide that you will start adopting that into your behaviors. Slow down your reactivity and be more mindful in that environment, much like how an empathetic person would respond. With consistent effort, that will shift your identity to being the empathetic one. Try experimenting with future memories, and begin to see and believe a new you is possible.

I'm containing this thought experiment within the family unit because the family is a relatively low-stakes and safe micro community that tolerates experimentation. If your family isn't a safe space, use the low-stakes community that is safest for you. Once you realize the process works in creating the future that you choose, you can then apply the practice to bigger things, such as a profession, companionship, or exploring your interests or ambitions.

Because this process occurs introspectively, future memories are a very internal form of exploration. Of course, this is not the only way you can explore your interests. You can also physically explore by traveling to the places that speak most loudly to your ambitions.

TRAVEL TO DESTROY PREJUDICE

When and where you are born gives you a specific context and life experience. Those contexts are limited in scope despite being helpful in developing your sense of identity. Ultimately, staying put limits your capacity.

When you explore the world outside of your origin, your changed context fills in the incomplete learning that gave rise to how you have prejudiced yourself, your interests, or what you perceive to be possible. When you travel, you are able to explore facts for yourself, experience new ideas, and acquire a fuller context for your prior knowledge. Over time, with more experience, you can move from being an armchair expert to a full-blown expert in your particular interests. J. R. R. Tolkien wrote, "Not all who wander are lost."* Rather, those who explore and wander find themselves.

In Hebrew, there is an oft-used phrase: *Shinui makom, shinui mazal.* It translates into English as "change your place, change your luck." Earlier in this chapter, we discussed that luck, as it is popularly applied, is something that can be cultivated. One way to create our own luck is by physically changing the context of our place. Distance doesn't matter. I'm not advocating that you travel to another country on the other side of the globe. You could, but that's not the specific point. It just needs to be 1) a place you haven't explored yet and 2) something that aligns with your interests and ambitions. When you travel, choose destinations that fit into your life's curriculum.

When your context of place is changed, your life trajectory changes as well. If you are or can be in control of your current place, that means you can also be in control of your current (and future) life trajectory. The people you come into contact with, the experiences you have, the lessons you learn, and all of the fruit from changing your context creates a new pattern of cultivated luck that will transform you into a new and improved person.

---

* J. R. R. Tolkien, *The Lord of the Rings: The Fellowship of the Ring* (New York: Houghton Mifflin, 1988), 182.

THE WONDER EFFECT

I ended up traveling at an early age. First, I decided to go to a school in Israel. After my studies there, I went to study in many different cities throughout the United States, including Los Angeles and New York. When in these places, I sought curious and supportive people because I wondered where the experience might lead. One decision can change your life, and several life-changing decisions can create a network of people who help you build your future life. At one point I had extensive conversations with Professor Marty Marshall of Harvard Business School and cultivated a mentoring relationship with him. He was one of the smartest minds in the country. I wasn't (and am not) some genius who was born to be business savvy. Rather, I traveled and, while traveling, used my interests and curiosity to cultivate opportunities. I worked at putting myself in the right place at the right time to make my luck less reliant on . . . well, luck.

Traveling helps with your creativity and personal growth. When you explore new places, you experience and interact with people who are different from you and do things in a way dissimilar to what you're used to. Experiencing those differences will change your thinking. Changing your thinking ends up changing your actions. Both will propel you forward and positively toward your ambitions.

As you change, those ideas that may have hampered your personal growth begin to erode. Where once limiting beliefs blocked and stifled your creativity and potential, travel opens you up to new ways of thinking and experiencing that inspire creativity and potential. Traveling is one of the best ways to change your context of place, for lack of a better word, and forces you into new experiences. However, if you cannot travel to your preferred destination at the moment, then you can "travel" through other means, such as books, music, and other media. Call it learning, call it reading, or call it whatever you want. You have the ability to take your five senses and give them different place inputs compared to the place you are in right now. Like the *Atlas Obscura*, there are excellent resources for readers to experience even the most nuanced obscurities of new places.

A big part of who you have become is a result of your experiences; therefore, it becomes necessary to seek new experiences if you want to be a different version of yourself or create a different future. It's like a chain, where each link leads to the next; it all compounds and is all connected.

ONE THING LEADS TO ANOTHER

Our biases are perpetuated relative to the amount of time we spend interacting with social media and its algorithms.* The way that it works with social media is that, when you choose

---

* Giovanni Luca Ciampaglia and Filippo Menczer, "Biases Make People Vulnerable to Misinformation Spread by Social Media," The Conversation, *Scientific American*, June 21, 2018, https://www.scientificamerican.com/article/biases-make-people-vulnerable-to-misinformation-spread-by-social-media/.

to click on certain content, you begin to see the same or similar content filtered to the top of your social media feed. That app's algorithm is designed to identify your interests and then feed you with more things related to that narrow focus to keep you engaged and sell your time to advertisers and inputs to information collectors. In this way, social media keeps your attention but limits what you would otherwise encounter, pigeonholing you into a specific set of ideas. That creates an echo chamber that is not beneficial to true exploration and growth.

However, you can use this structure in a positive way. What if you took that same structure, that same idea of the social media algorithm, but applied it to your own growth mindset and ability to explore your own interests and ambitions? What if you hijack yourself and start to pursue your interests on your own terms? We are back at one of the overall principles of *The Wonder Effect*. When you pull on a thread of interest, new threads appear for you to pull. By being wonder-minded and curious about what is possible, more positive growth occurs.

When you explore in the direction of your ambitions algorithmically, one "click" encourages more "clicks." When you experience the positives of growth, you may find that you have a yearning for more growth. When you realize that there is a growth algorithm of exploration, linking one success to the next becomes your normal state of mind: *Of course I am going to grow. Of course positive changes are*

EXPLORE ON YOUR OWN

possible. Of course my future is wider and brighter. Implementing an exploration algorithm, these will be your natural, ingrained thoughts rather than distant, I-wish-that-were-true hopes.

One thing leads to another. And linking positive, explorative experiences can happen at both the micro and macro level. Your daily micro exploration could be something as simple as trying new recipes as often as you can, opening you up to the world of culinary delights and adding another patch to your quilt. Your algorithmic macro exploration could include your frequent evaluation and resetting of achievable goals for your professional life. The possibilities are tremendous. When you have an exploratory attitude, you will find that you generate an ability to improvise positivity when one thing leads to the next, leading to important experiences and surprising results.

To illustrate these surprising moments of growth, I can recall a project I worked on in Connecticut. I was transforming a hotel into an apartment building. In this particular project, the rooms were relatively small and didn't provide the residents much opportunity for anything besides eating and sleeping. To solve this problem, I decided to build a series of amenities within the property, such as a theater, a workout room, a pool, and others. I had never done this before, so I was learning on the fly. (Or, to paraphrase Reid Hoffman, maybe I was learning how to build a plane while falling off of a cliff.)

In that exploratory process, I learned that I needed to source and manufacture specific parts to fit the building's unique shapes. When comparing costs, it turned out that manufacturing domestically was exorbitantly expensive, which led to some international travel. After a few stops, I ended up overseas and worked directly with the factory. Did I ever think to myself that building a pool would cause me to learn about manufacturing? Absolutely not. Did I think that learning about manufacturing would cause me to end up traveling internationally and working overseas? Another no from me. But, I had a clear direction, and my explorative desire to fulfill those ambitions caused a logical, positive, and achievable process of one thing leading to another. With each new link in the chain, I learned positive new skills and acquired important new experiences that shaped my future successes.

Among the things my story demonstrates is this important lesson: the unique mixture of experiences or contacts that your adventurous explorations provide are unique to you and completely change the course of your life's trajectory in a cultivated way. When one thing leads to another, you become a true explorer.

THE EXPLORER'S SPIRIT

Think back to the fable about the animal school. Recall that the structure of that school—the "system," if you will—was such that in the climbing class, the Eagle was punished for finding their own efficient route to the top of the tree that circumvented the actual need for climbing. The Eagle used aspects of their unique self to go beyond the limited scope of the animal school, believing that climbing the tree was the only route. As the fable is written, the Eagle demonstrated the spirit of an explorer by daring to change the school's context, finding a new mode of travel by which to achieve ambitions. If you see the value in pursuing new avenues to accomplish your goals such as the Eagle did, you also have an explorer's spirit. As you pursue, you might not actually end up accomplishing the thing that you set out to do, but you will learn more than you otherwise thought you would or could along the way and create an environment of manufactured luck. Following this exploratory process puts you in more positions to advance and prosper.

Exploring on your own terms, though, is the proverbial dipping of your toe into the pool of the selective unknown. It's the careful choice to put yourself in the direction of your life's curriculum and the beginning of a much deeper dive into your interests, ambitions, and goals. After getting comfortable with your explorer's spirit, you can then operate at a fast clip, growing yourself in an adventurous, exponential way. And while we have touched on the concept of being adventurous to some degree already, we must augment our spirit of exploration by fully immersing ourselves into the wondrous effects of adventure.

CHAPTER 5

BE ADVENTUROUS

A ship is safest in harbor, but that's not what ships are built for.

—JOHN G. SHEDD

Brandon Tseng, a former Navy SEAL and cofounder of Shield AI, is now known for developing US military drone technology. His goal was to assist soldiers with a myriad of tactical issues in modern warfare.* He was motivated by his own experiences. Among the tactical issues was the fatal funnel—the first soldier through a front door, uncertain if an enemy combatant with a loaded weapon was on the other side. Another issue Tseng wanted to address was to prevent the

---

* Elliot Ackerman, "A Navy SEAL, a Quadcopter, and a Quest to Save Lives in Combat," *WIRED*, October 30, 2020, https://www.wired.com/story/shield-ai-quadcopter-military-drone/.

destruction of military targets that housed unknown, innocent hostages inside. Similarly, Tseng thought, a drone could assist in confirming whether or not a target should be deemed a target. In one mission Tseng experienced, a soldier was just about to drop bombs on a building deemed a military target, but at the last moment, it was revealed to be a school. Tseng's experiences demonstrated a pattern of need that led him to his idea: scout drone technology. What if there was a quadcopter that could breach that first door, the so-called fatal funnel? What if there was a drone that could inspect a target to ensure there were no hostages inside or that it wasn't actually a school full of children? It seems like such an obviously good idea that others were probably working on it. In fact, Tseng believed that somebody would beat him to the punch. But to his surprise, he was the only one developing the technology.

For many years, drones had been in development for the military by companies such as Anduril and Skydio, the former being funded by billionaire tech investor Peter Thiel. Yet those companies were developing drones for other purposes, such as monitoring border crossings. It's as if these companies just assumed that the military was already using AI drone technology for fatal-funnel and interior-scouting purposes. But, of course, Tseng's visions for military drones didn't yet exist. And this remained true until Tseng completed development of his idea in 2015. Now, Shield AI has a defense contract with the United States for military drones that save the lives of many soldiers.

BE ADVENTUROUS

What lesson does Brandon Tseng's story teach us? Either there is nobody working on our specific, imaginative ideas, or they are working on them in a way that is different from our unique approach. Question the assumption that somebody is already doing it or that somebody else could do it better. Adventurously pursue your ideas with the confidence that you bring a unique perspective that will create a unique result. The maze of life often leads to dead-end walls where we mistakenly believe that our ambitions, interests, and imaginative ideas have already been done by somebody else. In fact, there is much more left to adventurously discover than we realize.

Being adventurous is, at its essence, taking the thought of *I can't* and transforming it into a simple, fundamental, and active question: *Why not?* Pursue an answer to that question with curiosity and rigor. Doing so will demonstrate to you that you can implement your ideas *and* that they are worth implementing. Act with conviction when experiencing something unfamiliar and interesting to you. Hold the belief that you can approach your idea uniquely. That belief is the baseline of living adventurously.

Building on that baseline, you also need to embrace discomfort to be adventurous. Many find the idea of adventure discomforting, as seeking out what's new will inevitably change what we have now. Perhaps there is a nostalgia to hang onto the present, but that type of thinking ultimately leads to a death of growth that is not too dissimilar to physical death. Accept that change is inevitable, that change can be a good thing, and that we are called on to be adventurous despite our discomfort.

FIND DISCOMFORT

Go beyond what you're comfortable with and settle into a different version of yourself. As Greek philosopher Heraclitus remarked, "The only constant in life is change."* With the busyness around us, his observation is especially accurate today. This means, if you are not comfortable with the fact that everything is nonstop and in constant flux, you will not be able to operate, grow, or adapt successfully. Therefore, it is crucial that you become comfortable with and open yourself to the discomfort of change. Doing so unlocks the possibilities of your future. In all honesty, to do anything else is to set a course for the slow erosion of yourself and your future.

Many hold a different view, of course. Occasionally, you may come across people who say, "I'm perfectly happy with where I am right now." For those who genuinely feel this way, we can be sincerely happy for them and hope they continue in this state. I believe in gratitude, and happiness for the present moment is one way to express our gratitude.

---

* Heraclitus quote, Arapahoe Libraries, https://arapahoelibraries.org/blogs/post/the-only-constant-in-life-is-change-heraclitus/.

BE ADVENTUROUS

However, feeling contentment to the point of stagnation makes us vulnerable to psychological atrophy.

Don't get the wrong image in your mind of a person in a hospital nightgown; psychological atrophy is much broader, and it suggests that the natural state of a given person's mental well-being will degrade slowly over time with disuse. In other words, for those who are perfectly happy with their life, without the conscious effort to grow and change from their present state, that happiness can only devolve into *less than* where they are right now.

By maintaining the status quo, the laws of inevitable change degrade contentment until it eventually disintegrates. It's impossible to remain in one way forever, and the cruel, obvious, and perhaps ironic twist for those who are statically content is that they will eventually change for the worse.

Because you cannot remain the same, it is up to you to determine how your change occurs. It's a bit of a red-pill/blue-pill situation a la *The Matrix*. For the person who thinks they are happy with what they have, they can prevent degradation by continually pushing for growth. How? Accept that to grow is to be comfortable with discomfort. Adventure freely into the unknown future with an exploratory and curious attitude, ready to approach new challenges energetically.

If this sounds challenging, it really isn't. Once you get the hang of it, it actually can be easy. But what does adventurously exploring the unknown look like? To prove it's easy, let's look at how children's video games demonstrate the basic principles of fearless adventure into uncharted waters.

A player boots up a game without any instructions, just a kid and a controller. They start playing and very quickly "die" by falling into this pit or being shot by that commando (or some such scenario). They keep running into the proverbial wall. Do they quit? Do they say, *Well, I'm happy with where I am right now*? Do they stop themselves because they are afraid they will continue to make mistakes or not figure out how to advance? No. They press on toward an end goal. They start the difficult level again, messing around with new button configurations and experimenting with a well-timed jump here, an enemy-avoiding dash there, and boom! They've climbed the insurmountable wall in front of them, perhaps calling their friends into the room to brag about their accomplishments.

For these video game players, obstacles serve as feedback. Defeats are seen as challenges to explore and overcome. Like the natural process of playing video games, you can road map and experiment with how you learn, grow, and generate comfort in that discomfort. The insurmountable walls that you face in your daily life, with adventurous experimentation, can be climbed and cleared.

But there's more to this video game analogy than meets the eye. With controllers in hand, these players enact playfulness as part of their growth-minded pursuit of the unknown. They play because they enjoy the process. You, too, must inject a similar joy and playfulness into your adventurous spirit. Joy breeds curiosity, and when you hit the inevitable walls in life, you should recognize that you were very close to clearing them. Feeling optimistic, you can then iterate in a different way and continually try new methods until you hit the perfectly timed "jump button" that helps you land clear of a given life obstacle.

When you pursue your interests with a playfulness that embraces discomfort, you ensure a journey on a feedback loop of constant growth potential. Play the video game of your life with energy and curiosity. This is the essential truth: you must adventurously wade into the uncomfortable unknown to achieve positive progress.

As you meet the challenges inherent in discomfort, you also foster the ability to get to know yourself in new, growth-minded ways.

KNOW YOURSELF IN NEW WAYS

Generally speaking, growth occurs when new knowledge and experience deepen your total and diverse understanding. Your wisdom deepens too. When you adventurously approach growth, the fear of the unknown is mitigated by excitement, even if you believe you are not ready for change. Adventuring into the unknown actually draws us into an opportunity to know ourselves in new ways.

The differences between the adventurer and the person who stays home are many. First, the person who refuses to explore outside of their daily routine accepts failure at face value. For them, obstacles act as a stopping point rather than a launching point. They think to themselves, *I don't need to take that risk,* without fully weighing all of the potential upsides. They let their anxious emotions override their sense of adventure and purpose.

The adventurer, on the other hand, opens themselves up to more vulnerability, holds their anxious emotions in check, and recognizes they have untapped potential. This vulnerability varies, of course. Emotional vulnerability and openness could emerge from a new, trusting relationship. Or the vulnerability of the adventurer could be physical. Think of those who are currently training to colonize and live on Mars for the first time in human history. They are not coming back from that adventure, and there is no guarantee of success, yet they are willing to put their mark on the pages of history—and risk discomfort.

Sticking with these brave Mars colonists for a moment, we must recognize that being bold and courageous pushes us beyond our limits. Intentionally living an adventurous life means embracing experiences to know yourself in new ways and to plumb the depths of your interests and ambitions. You become more whole when you are tasked to face something you've never faced before. How do you react? What does that say about you? The new experience will itself implicitly answer several questions for you, making you also aware of personal reservoirs of strength, creativity, and courage, and if not, it will show you where you may need additional scaffolding or guidance.

These depth-plumbing experiences can be both *intra*personal and *inter*personal. As your self evolves and emerges, people will begin to recognize the person you are becoming and, if they know you well, understand how your earlier traits naturally led to your growth. In time, new experiences will fuse with your being, and you will witness your own evolution. You will still be you, just a revised version. Getting to know yourself in a new way is natural, not artificial.

In the process of adventurous discovery, you will come to find that you either succeed or learn. It's a win-win scenario. That is to say, even if you do not succeed at something—in whatever measure may apply to a given situation—you will generate a new level of ease and understanding for that activity. That, in turn, opens up the space for becoming more experienced to prosper in the future. Continuing to add adventurous experiences transforms you into a different person and allows you to know yourself more fully.

You emerge.

This emerging can and should layer. Using the metaphor of a snowball, consider that it takes quite a bit of effort to get the initial snowball going. Once you get it rolling, only one or two tumbles will double or triple the original snowball's size. The same is true for adventure. After working toward the initial momentum of intentional adventure, you snowball and add layers to your self-understanding. "Adventure is out there," the character Charles said from the Pixar film *Up*.* And the sentiment is correct. Once you begin to seek it, you'll find it everywhere.

Fair warning: you may look back at your former self with embarrassment when you hit a certain growth threshold. *I explored so little and was so amateurish back then,* we might say about ourselves. If you listen to famous podcasters or follow any prominent YouTube channels, you have likely heard content creators discuss this phenomenon. They are mortified to look back at their earliest episodes to see their poor editing and equipment. And while there may be an objectively measurable difference in quality from where they started versus where they are now, they nonetheless layered their expertise over time within the adventure of their new medium. In fact, if you want to learn that one must adventurously get to know themselves to generate positive impacts and growth, binge-listen or binge-watch one of your favorite content creators' work. You will see (or hear) that they had to evolve adventurously into themselves and their expertise. They, like you, were once new to their craft and felt like an imposter.

---

* *Up*, Disney Pixar, directed by Peter Docter, screenplay by Bob Peterson. Disney-Pixar, May 2009.

BE ADVENTUROUS

MANAGE IMPOSTER SYNDROME

Everybody experiences imposter syndrome. I have some troubling news for you: there is little to no chance of overcoming this affliction. Notice that this section is titled "Manage," not "Cure." Imposter syndrome is not something that goes away. Even the greats among us, whoever you may consider them to be, experience imposter syndrome. Musician Harry Nilsson famously avoided live performances due to his inability to battle stage fright. Elsewhere, Dr. Adam Riess, Nobel laureate in physics, suffered from imposter syndrome even as he was accepting his Nobel Prize. When one accepts the Nobel Prize, they sign a book that includes the signatures of previous winners. Dr. Riess has said in interviews that seeing his name included with icons like Albert Einstein made him feel like he didn't belong. Even the greatest scientists on earth fall prey to imposter syndrome. It is inescapable.

On the other hand, it's kind of freeing to learn that we have no hope of overcoming it. We can accept it, live with it, and act *in spite* of it. If you are feeling imposter syndrome as you adventurously pursue new experiences, it is more than okay. It also probably means you're on the right path. Going back to the video game metaphor, it is often said within the video game community that if you encounter enemies within the game, you are probably going the right way. Imposter syndrome is that enemy, so to speak, that means you are headed in the right direction and wading into the adventurous unknown. Never let the obstacle of imposter syndrome prevent you from being great.

Funny thing is, I feel imposter syndrome doesn't go away; it just gets lessened until you venture into new things. I felt undeserving to be in my Harvard Business School classes. I felt everyone else was really deserving based on their backgrounds. However, I'm deeply curious, I worked hard, I asked tons of questions, and I ended up feeling like my place was justified. This was true when I first got into real estate as well. In listening to so many podcasts of those who also started from scratch, the common denominator was *persistence*.

TO BE BIG OR TO BE GREAT?

There is a well-known dichotomy in the business world separating how public and private companies make decisions. In public companies, there is regular reporting, typically at quarterly intervals. This report and those who read it are worried about the stock price above all other factors. Because the focus is to maximize the stock price for each regular report, short-term gain becomes the motivating factor when making business decisions. This approach often depreciates the value of the stock's potential in the long run because short-term decisions have unforeseen consequences. Private companies tend to look at the bigger picture and

BE ADVENTUROUS

pursue strategies that might look harsh in the short term but eventually pay off.

Amazon was and is a prime example of long-game planning. Like him or hate him, Jeff Bezos is the epitome of the businessperson who knew that pursuing a long-term strategy would pay massive dividends later rather than sooner. For three years he kept the company private, and it never saw profit. And even after it went public, Bezos maintained his long-term vision in the early years of the company and ignored investor complaints for short-term success. It took eight years before the first miniscule profits were realized. Twenty years after Amazon first reported profits, as we all know, it has transformed into one of the biggest corporations in the world.

Stock-price-chasing companies look to make their price as *big* as possible between reports. In contrast, long-term companies seek to make a company as *great* as possible. So, the question emerges, do you want to be big, or do you want to be great? Maximizing the benefits of adventure means having the long-term ambitions of your life's curriculum in mind and not living for the short term. Recall our discussion about setting goals. Ideally, your short-term goals are designed to specifically accomplish your long-term goals. Keeping the long game in mind is the path to becoming great.

The concept of forgoing bigness in favor of greatness reminds me of Michael Gerber's book *The E-Myth Revisited*. There, he argues that professional success means working *on* your business while you are working *in* your business.* If I were to translate that through my way of thinking, this means you can develop your life while you are living your life. So, for those of us who require many short-term concessions to keep a roof over our heads—earning money at that lower-paying job, barely having enough to make ends meet, and everything else—we will have to put in more precise and consistent micro effort in order to go after a bigger, long-term goal. Maybe that includes saving money or reinvesting how you spend your off-hours time. It just depends on the particular circumstances. But if you want to break out of the short-term cycle, at the very least, you will need to take small steps toward your greater future. Incremental improvement will build on itself and create the change you are looking for.

It might not be your fault that you find yourself in a deficit, but it is your problem. Be mindful of your immediate choices, and ask yourself whether or not they help you be big or be great. The go-to strategy for making greatness a regular part of your life is to practice being extraordinary.

PRACTICE BEING EXTRAORDINARY

Being extraordinary is such an abstract concept when you think about it. However, we can get a grounded understanding

---

* Michael E. Gerber, *The E-Myth Revisited: Why Most Small Businesses Don't Work and What to Do About It* (New York: HarperCollins, 1995), 116–133.

of it. This chapter has highlighted the importance of bravely facing discomfort, adventurously experiencing new things, cultivating a new and whole self, and being great. Brave. Adventurous. Unique. Great. These are not words that describe somebody who is ordinary. On the contrary, they describe somebody who is remarkable and extraordinary. Choose behaviors that exhibit the meaning implied in the word *extraordinary* by being more than ordinary, even if only incrementally.

From that understanding, you need to continuously practice at being one more step beyond ordinary. Why do I say "practice" and not "be"? Because where you are going in the future is never in the here and now. If you think you have everything right here and are satisfied, then you will never get *there* (your ambitions for the future). So, by framing extraordinary behavior as a practice, you are emphasizing the importance of incremental improvements that sustain growth in perpetuity. "I can always be *more* extraordinary." The more you practice being extraordinary, the more you become extraordinary.

SPACE FOR SERENDIPITY

The space for serendipity means being humble enough and open enough to realize there are infinite possibilities to arrive at the same destination. With this mindset, the obstacles may mean a detour or challenge that needs to be overcome in order to develop the capacities needed to move up to the next level. It's really seeing things as they are, which I believe is inherently mysterious. Consider the developments in physics like Heisenberg's uncertainty principle, which states that nothing can be predicted with certainty but only degrees of probability, even those things you think are obvious or take for granted, like an action that generates a reaction.

It's like choosing to see gravity as that which holds you back from flying (OCD goal setting mindset) versus gravity being the very awesome force that provides the perfect tension that allows your muscles to develop and not atrophy so that you can live a terrestrial life.

Stephen Covey's famous book, *The 7 Habits of Highly Effective People*, explains how our own lack of adventure gets us into trouble. Covey says that if you are trying to climb a ladder—such as a corporate ladder—to pursue your ambitions and goals, it will be detrimental to your climb if, when you get to the top, you find the ladder leaning against the wrong house.* Being too focused on a particular goal might prevent you from seeing where that ladder leads. Controlling every small detail may help you toward a goal, but it may also create a myopic resistance to experiences that may lead to you jumping to a better, taller, or different ladder. Be persistent

---

* Stephen R. Covey, *The 7 Habits of Highly Effective People* (New York: Simon & Schuster, 2020), 95–97.

BE ADVENTUROUS

in being open to where your passions take you. With your wonder-minded self, be curious and reflect on how one thing could lead to another. That passion and wondrous drive will create serendipitous results.

Passion and persistence are two major pillars of *The Wonder Effect*. You lose sight of what's ahead when you lose your passion and persistence. Both traits give you the ability to lift your head, see the big picture, and create space for serendipity. The excitement that emanates from adventurous thinking keeps you open to new possibilities. It gets your mind thinking opportunistically and with a desire to try new things.

I'll give you a personal example. Recently, I've become obsessed with personal eVTOL (electric vertical take-off and landing) machines. I'm talking about the ones you get in and actually fly. Some of the most amazing versions can cost north of $100,000. I started thinking, *If I would love to fly this really cool thing, then other people probably feel the same way.* All of a sudden, I found myself adventurously envisioning ways I could get that way-too-expensive drone within reach of the public. Perhaps I could reach out to the manufacturer of the drone, generate a licensing agreement, and set up locations where people would pay affordable fees to fly in an eVTOL around beautiful, hard-to-reach vistas. Guests could experience landmarks in new ways. Imagine experiencing the Grand Canyon, the White Mountains, Crater Lake, the Palouse, Multnomah Falls, the Na Pali Coast, Horseshoe

Bend, and many landmarks in distinctly new ways. In all honesty, this is a cash-cow idea. I mean, I would pay a company to fly the eVTOL in one of these spaces.

At the time of writing, there are no businesses doing this, so if the idea still hasn't been taken by the time of publishing, you can have that business idea for free, or reach out to me and we'll work on it together. Personally, eVTOLs are just an interest of mine. I am currently busy with my present projects and haven't prioritized any development of a business surrounding the licensing of eVTOLs. But because of my life's quilt and a mind shaped by *The Wonder Effect*, my openness and adventurousness create a space for serendipity where I can tinker with the new possibilities that emanate from my interests.

When you start creating the space for serendipity, you will find that your ambitions and goals transform from distant dreams into achievable experiences and/or attainable business models. In other words, Paulo Coelho was right when he wrote that once you make a decision, "all the universe conspires to make it happen."*

With any serendipitous adventure, there will be obstacles. There is even a strong chance that as you were reading my eVTOL-licensing idea, you had various red flags pop into your mind like, *would parks even allow a private business to fly eVTOLs?* or *What would the insurance look like?* Those are

---

* Paulo Coelho, *The Alchemist* (San Francisco: HarperOne, 1993), 24.

great questions or, rather, obstacles that arise in the course of adventurous thinking. But there are ways to categorize and address these problems to continue moving forward.

LIMINAL SPACE AND TECHNICAL VS. ADAPTIVE PROBLEMS

What is liminal space? It is a space between—neither here nor there. It is journeying through the unknown, where all positive growth and transformation occurs. Famously, and biblically, the Jewish people journeyed from Egypt to Israel to settle there. Along the way, they existed in a liminal space between start and end. The creation of the Jewish people took place in this no-man's-land. They were a slave people before they were taken out of Egypt. While being nowhere, or more precisely *in the desert for forty years*, they became themselves. Only then could they arrive at their intended destination. In other words, they became who they needed to be in order to arrive at where they were intending to go.

For your own journey, as was the case with the Jewish people, adventuring into the unknown through liminal space is, by definition, a vulnerable place to be. There, you will encounter many obstacles, challenges, and lessons on your way to knowledge and wisdom. In a parallel way, you may experience being nowhere, or nowhere near where you want to be or become. But that is precisely the space where your growth occurs and where you will emerge to become the person who is capable of arriving at your intended destination, physical or otherwise.

As has been established, we live in a world that discourages us from pursuing our distinct and different future. As a side note, I think this is simply because stasis, familiarity, and constants feel safe, and the world wants to stay safe; therefore it wants you to stay the same. But if we come to terms with growth occurring in the "dangers" of liminal space, we can mitigate the effects of the world's discouragement.

Liminal space is the threshold between success and failure. Just like the threshold to a door, it provides an opportunity to enter or exit; change is either accepted or not. It puts you in a place of uncertainty. It's not a given that you shouldn't continue, but the important thing is to continue forward. It bears repeating: liminal space is where all positive growth and transformation occurs. You may think the fears we experience while facing challenges are daunting, but they actually keep us composed and focused.

The Wonder Effect is an ongoing philosophy of being open and willing to change via new experiences. In that spirit, another way you can positively adventure into the unknown is by framing your world as a series of solvable technical and adaptive problems. Technical problems are those obstacles that have an external solution. Think about the technical problems that caused the Boeing 737 MAX crashes. In both crashes, there was an external technical issue with a sensor that, when identified, had a technical solution. Once the solution was discovered, it was implemented.

In adaptive problems, *you* are your own obstacle. The only solution to an adaptive problem is for you to change. If, for example, your doctor told you that you had an unhealthily large BMI and risked serious illness without a change in your diet and an increase of exercise, you would have to make new choices and become a different person to implement the solution. You would have to adapt. As it pertains to pursuing your ambitions, interests, and goals, the adaptive problems you face could be varied and multifaceted. Perhaps you believe you don't have enough time for new experiences. If so, then you need to adapt by taking a time inventory to determine where in your schedule you could make room for your new adventures.

A NEW ADVENTURE, ALWAYS

If you want something different, you have to be different. Being adventurous with your interests means that you seek growth, change, and a desire to learn new depths of your possible self. When you are open to these things, you will find that your new experiences will bestow small bits of wisdom on you as you become ever closer to being extraordinary.

Over time, those small bits of wisdom change you for the better and lead to progress. That is what happened to Thomas

Edison, who attempted to perfect the filament to make a commercial success of the light bulb. He waded through 2,774 failed experiments before getting it right. Undoubtedly, that process was one of deduction where different inputs, variables, and components were put together. Trying one way after another, he could use his experiments to infer what might lead to greater success for the next experiment. If a horse's hair didn't work as a filament, it was unlikely that other types of animal hair—things of a similar property—would work, and he could eliminate a large set of possible experiments going forward. And there we are at the phrase "going forward" again. That's the incredible lesson of being adventurous: always move forward. Edison's adventurous pursuit of the light bulb required failure to modulate his experiment until success was found. He iterated himself in different ways until he changed the world.

You should never stop seeking new experiences and places, especially in the face of failure. There will be setbacks along the way. Those failures create a certain tension that can motivate your journey to continue from a new angle. The elasticity of tension, like a rubber band, propels you forward.

CHAPTER 6

EMBRACE FAILURE

I'm not telling you it's going to be easy. I'm telling you it's going to be worth it.

—ARTHUR L. WILLIAMS JR.

Although nominated for the Nobel Prize in 2014, Dr. Brian Keating's famous and groundbreaking BICEP (background imaging of cosmic extragalactic polarization) experiment failed to net him the status of Nobel laureate. Failing to win the Nobel Peace Prize—the most prestigious award in science—must be a spirit-crushing burden and career blackmark, right? In response to this experience, Dr. Keating turned something many perceive as a negative into an objectively positive success. By pursuing and then failing to win the Nobel Prize, Dr. Keating created the capacity for personal growth that, in many ways, outshined any accolades associated with winning the award. His greatest failure became his greatest success.

After his loss, Dr. Keating became fascinated by the Nobel Prize itself, including its history and how the winners are determined. He began to inquire further. What does it actually mean to win the Nobel Prize? As he researched, he found that, in his analysis of the facts, the prize does a lot to both benefit and restrict the pursuit of scientific knowledge. All of that work came to fruition with the publication of his book, *Losing the Nobel Prize: A Story of Cosmology, Ambition, and the Perils of Science's Highest Honor*.

His insights created a massive conversation about the machinations of the science industry and how it has many flaws that discourage our scientific imagination—flaws beyond just the Nobel Prize. Following the success of his book, industry-insider conversations emerged. Dr. Keating, as the lead voice in these conversations, was in demand. He created a podcast, among other ventures, to continue the conversation for the scientific community. Shortly thereafter, the podcast blew up and transcended the scientific community. Entering into pop culture, his podcast now acts as an inspirational sounding board for everyday people looking to rethink their limiting beliefs about failure. In many ways, Dr. Keating now has more influence than the person who bested him for the Nobel Prize.

Dr. Keating's Nobel Prize "loss" was actually a net win. When Nelson Mandela famously said, "I never lose. I either win or learn,"* his characterization of failure aligns with Dr. Keating's experience. When the "loss" came down, Dr. Keating responded by embracing failure, which included learning and adapting. When it was all over, he reinvented himself and became a bigger success than he originally hoped.

And although Dr. Keating's losing the Nobel Prize was quite dramatic, not all of our failures happen on such a scale. We all face failure daily. Further, it accumulates. Sometimes residual failure builds until we find ourselves in the middle of an emotional outburst because we forgot that we have to stop for gas on the way to work. In other words, there is a dichotomy between built-up small failures and big failures. They can both have the same result, which is to brand us with the feeling of failure.

Failure can easily overwhelm us. So how do we combat invisible, everyday failure? The same way we combat our biggest failure: by embracing it. To experience growth and success, you must embrace two facts about failure: 1) it is inevitable and consistent and 2) it is necessary for learning. Despite these truths, failure can still hurt.

THE STING OF FAILURE

Our desire to avoid failure manifests from our desire to avoid pain. That desire, though, is misplaced. The simple truth is

---

* Nelson Mandela quote, Goodreads, Inc. 2024, https://www.goodreads.com/quotes/9041891-i-never-lose-i-either-win-or-learn.

that we've all been failing all of our lives. What's more, anything that might constitute a success was built from failure. Therefore, the sting of failure is actually a precursor to success.

Think about it. Failure has been responsible for our successes since day one. Babies construct their own resiliency and learning through failure. They don't decide one day to simply go from sitting to walking. Inspired by the movements of the adults around them, they experiment with little wiggles in their legs and arms. Would you tell a baby they're a failure and shouldn't try to walk because their wiggles weren't getting the job done? Of course not. After realizing they can wiggle, babies try balancing and shuffling. A few weeks later, they are scooting. Perhaps a month goes by and then they crawl. No point thus far in the progression can be described as successful walking. Each of these steps is, in fact, a failure to walk. Are their efforts adorable? Yes. Are their efforts walking? Afraid not. A baby learning to walk is really a long series of failures. Yet eventually, and despite the setbacks, the baby *will* walk. Failure is, in fact, the first thing you ever experienced and is still your most frequent teacher.

With these facts in mind, consider the next time you are touched with the sting and pain of failure. Recall that your entire identity is designed to fail forward into becoming. This recognition, however, is rarely enough to address our negative response to failure. If failure is ingrained and necessary to our growth and survival, then why can it feel so

EMBRACE FAILURE

shameful? The answer goes back to our first chapter and the cultural myths that are given to us externally, often by so-called experts. Myths become imbued in our identity. As we learned, we can thankfully disentangle them from us.

Failure is absolutely shunned in our society, especially as we are growing up. We learn to be so afraid of failure that, as adults, most of us view our own successful lives as failures. Rabbi Jonathan Sacks observed that, when surveyed, 40 percent of successful people did not believe they were successful, and as many as 70 percent felt that way at some point or another during their lives.* Yet these people were not failures. We seem to look at where we are not perfect and extrapolate those supposed failures to our totality, carrying some type of shame or failure avoidance.

Why are we trained to avoid failure at all costs? Perhaps it's our school system. When you take a test, let's say you get 60 percent, and that counts as a failing grade. Instead of the reductive label of "failing," learning 60 percent of the material tells you quite a bit. First, it gives you the missing data points that you still need to learn. In other words, it identifies your next opportunity. Second, you learned more than half of the material, which is quite a lot. Third, you can identify that you have the space and reason to grow. One would

---

* Rabbi Jonathan Sacks, "The Greatest Success Is to Help Others Succeed," BBC Radio 4, April 7, 2011, https://rabbisacks.org/archive/the-greatest-success-is-to-help-others-to-succeed/.

think that a student earning 60 percent, moving forward, would then be tasked to learn the 40 percent of material missed. None of that occurs though. Instead, you are labeled a "failure." Labeling students as failures perpetuates fixed and unimaginative mindsets for an entire society.

School is a feedback loop designed to define failure as a bad thing. The social consequences of academic failure are terrible. When we create a social institution that combines the feeling of failure with public shame, we are teaching our kids to steer clear of the failures inherent in growth-minded experiences. A child brought up in a failure-shaming system lives their life understanding failure as a sign of weakness instead of necessary for building strength. It is a tragic inverse of a school's intention to nurture the child's growing brain.

Bad grades. Good grades. That is our system. What we don't consider is that somebody who gets "good grades" may not actually be doing well. Perhaps they are not being challenged and their potential is being limited. Somebody with "good grades" could actually be a student the school is passively holding back and damaging, which is not something to celebrate. For those with "bad grades," they are being told that their observable room for improvement is something they should be ashamed of. Those judgments then inform a sense of feeling prejudiced, which then informs a lifelong sense of feeling like everything we do is valued through whether or not we "failed."

EMBRACE FAILURE

The sting of failure we carry need not be damaging to our emotional well-being. If, as I argued earlier, failure is actually the precursor of success, we need to learn how we can turn our failures into success much in the same way Dr. Keating did.

TURN THE GRAPES OF PAIN INTO WINE

The first step to turning your failures into successes is to reframe your understanding, as you have been doing. Does understanding failure as a necessary experience make it painless? Absolutely not. But it does reduce the negative emotional impact. Our weaknesses make us human, messy, and complex. Wrestling with our weaknesses strengthens our resolve against failure. If you are skeptical of what I just said, stay with me. I'm about to detail the process of emotional reframing.

The same principle that governs our emotions also holds true with physical pain. If you were told that you had to have surgery without anesthesia to survive the operation, you could understand that intellectually, but it wouldn't reduce the pain of being under the knife. However, that awareness would change how you *experience* the pain. Consider the options. If you weren't informed of the need to operate without anesthesia, you might experience the surgical pain as torture or an attack. When made to understand that the pain is necessary for surgical success, the pain wouldn't carry that additional feeling of violence against your person. Your emotional well-being would be less impacted.

Failure works similarly in that the emotional stings we suffer from falling short are mitigated when we embrace it as a necessary step in the process toward success. We may fail thousands of times, as Edison did, but our capacity to fail into more successes increases with greater emotional health. Ultimately, this emotional reframing is what it will take to change our lives for the better.

It can serve our understanding to look at the winemaking process. Humans are messy, just like the process of making wine. Originally, wine was made by throwing grapes into a vat. A person would enter the vat to stomp the juices out. If you can believe it, this process actually has a name; it's called grape-treading. While grape-treading, the grape gets crushed. Imagine for a moment that you are the grape.

Getting crushed feels painful. Losing its juice, a crushed grape seems like something messy and worthless just occurred. You got stepped on. But over time, the original juice doesn't become less worthy. The opposite occurs. It ferments into a fine wine. Your "getting crushed" experiences are fermenting lessons; they transform you from a grape into wine. By getting crushed, you are actually extracting the elements that will help you transform into something of even more value and greatness.

This wine metaphor shows us the importance of failure. Initially, Dr. Keating's Nobel Prize loss may have been like

EMBRACE FAILURE

grape juice stains on his clothing for the world to see. But over time, the juice he produced from his scientific career fermented into the wine that is his new, influential role as author and researcher. The so-called stains that failure leaves behind are actually evidence of the fruits of our labor.

When you feel crushed—when you experience a certain level of pain or failure—it provides the juice and motivation to turn those grapes of pain into wine. By mitigating the sting of failure in this way, you can become comfortable with the fact that success is just around the corner.

FIND REASSURANCE IN THE PARETO PRINCIPLE

The Pareto principle is one way we can approach a new understanding of failure. Named after economist and political scientist Vilfredo Pareto and widely used, the principle generally argues that 80 percent of all successes are the result of 20 percent of efforts.* This principle is highly transferable to all aspects of our lives. For example, if you run a business, it is a common business rule that 80 percent of your income comes from 20 percent of your customers. In my business of real estate, I can attest to this principle, as 80 percent of my earnings come from 20 percent of my best properties. But

---

* Erika Rasure, "What Is the Pareto Principle: aka the Pareto Rule or 80/20 Rule?" Investopedia, March 2024, https://www.investopedia.com/terms/p/paretoprinciple.asp

this principle seems to play out in situations not tied to businesses and profits, such as professional sports. In many major sports, a few elite players can create the majority of a team's success.

Now, let's step back from this principle and look at it from a top-down view. If most of our success comes from a very small portion of our work, that means that the majority of our work—around 80 percent—is bearing little fruit. In a traditional sense, that work might be labeled an abject failure, which can be overwhelming. If overwhelmed, it's much easier to quit pursuing a given interest or ambition altogether.

The way it's traditionally written about, you will hear folks argue that you need to focus on and ratchet the 20 percent (while neglecting the 80 percent) to get more from the 80 percent "profits" it produces. While I believe that can be an important strategy, I want to add a new reading of the principle to unlock your perspective on failure. Embrace the 80 percent of your work that yields only 20 percent of your results because that failure will teach you what you need to do to ratchet-up your successes. All of your work is important. Anyone who says 80 percent of your work is a failure negatively misconstrues its vital importance. Using *The Wonder Effect* and a wonder-minded approach, see that this 80 percent helps make all of your pursuits possible. Pulling all of your threads of interest creates an atmosphere of positive growth.

EMBRACE FAILURE

To instill yourself with courage and dedication, you need to reframe your understanding of failure. Get comfortable with the idea that 80 percent of your work will yield very few positive results. That is normal, and it is the way it goes for everybody. You are not failing. You are laying the foundation for your successes. *All* of the work is important, even the so-called failures. Doing *all* of the work enables you to generate the 20 percent of efforts that create 80 percent of your successes. Using the Pareto principle, you can continue to act in the face of challenges and failures to maintain the momentum required to achieve your greatest successes.

I can sense that some of you are reading about the Pareto principle and thinking, *This can't be universal. I know lots of people whose every effort translates into wild success.* When successful people fill our screens and news feeds, we fall into the trap of comparing and despairing. Think of celebrity culture. Be they actors, entrepreneurs, influencers, talking heads, or anything else, the general population only encounters celebrities at very specific and premeditated moments. Maybe in a film they made, an interview, or a news story about them. To us normal people, celebrities must be living this around-the-clock wave of success, where every minute of every day drips with efficiency and prosperity. But what we see is actually only a part of their life that exists within the 20 percent of their efforts. They spend so much time behind the scenes working to make those brief moments and appearances possible. There's an odd irony that, in following our favorite celebrities on social media platforms like Instagram, we compare our lives to theirs. This comparison is unhealthy because—even if their lives were being accurately depicted, which they are not—it's not the correct methodology to pursue or achieve what we're looking for. Their meticulously constructed celebrity personality is only the tip of a much larger iceberg of their experience.

Consider Dwayne "The Rock" Johnson. Each year, he is among the highest paid actors. He's charming and funny in interviews. He has great range as an actor, successfully appearing in action films, comedy films, and dramas. When we see him in these circumstances, it seems like he has incredible success with such ease. But he works incredibly hard and faces daily challenges to maintain his success. Just to name one behind-the-scenes challenge he faces, let's look at his grueling diet and exercise regimen. It includes an enormous amount of particulars. To give you an idea, it has been reported that he eats two-and-a-half pounds of cod a day for protein. He also exercises around four hours a day. Does he get paid to work out? Does he get paid to eat cod? No. In fact, he has to pay quite a bit for chefs and personal trainers. Eating and working out are not the areas where he sees the fruits of his labor. Acting is where he generates his success. But, and this is a big but, he would not be a famous actor if he didn't work hard to give himself those opportunities. Eighty percent of his work generates the ability to film movies 20 percent of the time. Like us, celebrities live by the Pareto principle.

EMBRACE FAILURE

Reframe your own life through the Pareto principle. Understand that, to obtain the 20 percent of work that leads to the bulk of your success, you must build a foundation of 80 percent of efforts that seemingly have no returns tied to them. Understanding this improves our ability to stay motivated in the face of perceived failure.

Where there is immense success, there is also immense failure. It is no accident that the best power hitters in baseball also top the list for most strikeouts in history. All of the top-ten career strikeout leaders were home-run heroes. They include Hall-of-Famer Reggie Jackson, as well as Sammy Sosa and Alex Rodriguez. Even Babe Ruth, the original home-run superstar with nicknames like "Sultan of Swat" and "The Big Bam" led the league in strikeouts five times throughout his career. Ruth's penchant for strikeouts earned him another of his many nicknames: The King of Strikeouts. Of course, folks only remember his favorable nicknames and accolades. He and others like him didn't stop trying to hit home runs because of their massively high failure rate. Instead, they kept swinging for the fences, comfortable with the failure that gave them the opportunity to generate success. As NHL player Wayne Gretzky famously said, "I miss one hundred percent of the shots I don't take."*

---

* Wayne Gretzky quote, Goodreads, Inc. 2024, https://www.goodreads.com/quotes/4798-you-miss-one-hundred-percent-of-the-shots-you-don-t.

WELCOME FEAR, NOT PANIC

I was able to meet former Navy SEAL Robert O'Neill, the soldier responsible for killing Osama bin Laden. He often speaks about the importance of fear. When speaking publicly, listeners frequently ask some version of this question: "Were you afraid during the mission that ended bin Laden's life?" In one of these responses, his exact reply was, "Without fear, there isn't courage."* He argued that fear kept him alive and composed enough to carry out the order to kill bin Laden.

A certain level of fear creates situational and heightened awareness that makes certain, regardless of your pursuits, you are crossing every *t* and dotting every *i*. You are still composed, asking the right questions, seeking solutions, and attempting to overcome obstacles. In other words, fear generates the necessary fuel to approach a situation with open eyes. You are ready to learn and absorb as much as possible to mitigate risks. It opens you up to explore with curiosity, adventure, and a welcome attitude toward failure.

Phobias and panic paralyze us from making forward progress. Panic shuts down our problem-solving, imaginative, and curious brain. We become emotionally flooded, which leads to a complete freak-out spurred by our limiting

---

* Rose Lane, "The Navy SEAL Who Killed Osama Bin Laden: NEVER QUIT," *OKC Friday*, September 24, 2021, https://okcfriday.com/the-navy-seal-who-killed-osama-bin-laden-never-quit-p16461-92.htm.

EMBRACE FAILURE

beliefs. Panic and phobias blind us to the opportunities of the Pareto principle. In the case of a Navy SEAL like Robert O'Neill, he said, "Fear keeps you alive, panic gets you killed."* O'Neill ascertained that had he panicked during his mission, he would have revealed his position to the enemy and become another killed-in-action (KIA) statistic.

How do you know if you are experiencing motivational fear or debilitating panic? Phobias and panic are completely psychological and have no basis in reality. They are your misdirected imagination telling yourself a story that's not real, suffocating you with the imagined negative implications of every terrible scenario that could play out. Unfortunately, these fake stories have real consequences for our emotional well-being and prevent us from acting with a growth mindset. Phobias panic your mind into paralysis and, at best, lead to poor decision-making.

Fear, on the other hand, is something that focuses our mind toward positive growth. As with failure, reframe your understanding of fear's role. Persistence is the key to embracing failure for the purpose of positive growth.

PERSISTENCE PAYS OFF

The thirtieth president of the United States, Calvin Coolidge, made this remark about persistence:

---

* Robert O'Neill quote, Goodreads, Inc. 2024, https://www.goodreads .com/quotes/3177180-fear-can-keep-you-alive-the-trick-is-not-to.

Nothing in this world can take the place of persistence. Talent will not; nothing is more common than unsuccessful men with talent. Genius will not; unrewarded genius is almost a proverb. Education will not; the world is full of educated derelicts. Persistence and determination alone are omnipotent. The slogan "Press On!" has solved and always will solve the problems of the human race.*

I equate persistence to continuity. The things that we value in our lives are the result of persistence and continuity. If you noticed, Coolidge argued the same thing when he used the word "always." One cannot be persistent for a finite amount of time, stop their pursuit, then become persistent again. It must be continuous and constant. Think of persistence like your need for oxygen. If you stopped breathing, you would die. You can't just stop breathing for a while. There is a continuous need to breathe; therefore we maintain persistent effort—even if that effort is subconscious—to breathe. Persistence requires continuity.

Without persistence, we create an arrested development, and in some cases an atrophy in our lives. For that baby at the beginning of the chapter learning to walk, if they didn't

---

* *Oxford Reference*, "Calvin Coolidge 1872–1933," accessed June 30, 2022, https://www.oxfordreference.com/view/10.1093/acref/9780191826719.001.0001/q-oro-ed4-00003260.

persistently defy failure, their legs would atrophy, stop developing, and they would be immobile their entire lives.

I always say that persistence, or lack thereof, will determine which direction our life egg is broken—from within or without. That might sound like an unusual metaphor, but stay with me. Does the egg break from the inside or the outside? Without growth through persistence, it breaks from the outside, cracked open by some force or entity to scramble our growth and development. If, on the other hand, we maintain persistence and grow inside our egg, our efforts will lead to our incubating egg breaking from the inside. Having matured, like a baby chick poking through their shell, we've given ourselves the ability to break out of our shell and open up into a new world of wonder.

We face pressure from all directions, but it will be our persistence that allows us to break from the inside and to emerge in a state of growth mindedness. Either you're going to grow out of your current egg, or you're going to get crushed. These two options follow what's known as the entropy principle.

The layman's version of the entropy principle is as follows. Without persistence to grow, the nature of matter is that things will degrade into chaos or disorder. So which direction do you want to go? You can either push from the inside with persistence to grow outward, or let yourself be pushed from the outside to degrade into chaos. If you decide not to pursue your adventure, pressure will be applied from the outside that stalls your growth. The more you are persistent in the face of failure, the more your growth is inevitable and the more you break from the inside.

Furthermore, your persistent growth opens you up to complex new adventures. That's right, even our failures can lead us into new directions, as Dr. Keating demonstrated to us at the top of this chapter. Our failures give rise to new beginnings, something called a happy accident.

HAPPY ACCIDENTS

One powerful method to redefining failure is to understand these events or moments as happy accidents. In the pursuit of a given ambition or goal, the unintended result can be framed as either positive or negative. You have the sole choice on how you characterize the challenges you face. Are they negative failures or positive learning opportunities?

On a recent trip with my daughter to the Mark Twain House and Museum in Hartford, Connecticut, we participated in a painting activity. Despite my not being artistically inclined, I was aiming for realism. In the course of tightly gripping my brush as I formed my tableau, my elbow tipped a bowl of paint all over my canvas. Whoops! After we both composed ourselves from laughter, she referred to it as a happy accident.

We honestly didn't mind the expressionist splotches that remained. It was unusual, abstract, and took the pressure off the need for realism. I changed directions and created a fun and imaginative impression, something we quite enjoyed. This anecdote reveals that spilling paint—what might otherwise be perceived as a flaw or failure—actually *added* value. In life, you will spill paint in everything you do. When that happens, use it to your advantage. Maximize the effects of the happy accidents. For example, not only did I like my painting better, but the time I had with my daughter was made more memorable.

That a flaw could add value is a truth you can observe in many arenas. Consider collectors who pursue memorabilia. Let's say there are two Steven Spielberg director's chairs up for auction. They have much less objective value compared to a normal chair because director's chairs are not terribly comfortable or functional. So, they are already flawed in that sense. But let's say one is in pristine condition (sat in once), and the other has ink stains, some type of mustard from a sandwich that Spielberg ate one day, and a cut mark from Spielberg's watch scraping the wood. Having a stained and damaged chair seems like it would be the worse and more flawed chair.

As it turns out, that second chair would fetch a much higher price than the pristine chair. The collector would get excited about the implications of the flaws. Perhaps the ink stains signal Spielberg making last-minute notes in the script before shooting. In that sense, the chair is a piece of historical importance. The flaws in the chair are actually proof of Spielberg's successes.

The same is true for our own lives. Most of the things we consider as flaws or failures—the "ink stains" in plain sight that make us look unusable—are the same happy accidents that shape our life quilt, generate our strengths, and prove our successes.

When you embrace failure by reframing it as a happy accident, you tell yourself that you've created an entirely new dynamic. You can work with and use so-called failure as a launch pad for more adventurous exploration. This mindset shift creates *The Wonder Effect*, where what was once considered negative is transformed into something positive, impactful, motivational, creative, and open. When the redefinition of failure is combined with a persistent pursuit of ambitions, happy accidents will lay bare new and dramatic possibilities for growth.

FAILURE IS NECESSARY

Researcher and author Jim Collins made the case that failure is actually necessary for greatness and crucial to understanding the limitlessness of hope:

> The signature of the truly great vs. the merely successful is not the absence of difficulty. It's the ability to come back from setbacks, even cataclysmic catastrophes, stronger than before. Great nations can decline and recover. Great companies can fall and recover.

EMBRACE FAILURE

Great social institutions can fall and recover. And great individuals can fall and recover. As long as you never get entirely knocked out of the game, there remains hope.*

There are several things we can glean from Collins here. First, putting yourself in new and difficult situations isn't the only requirement for greatness. Another determining factor for greatness is the gumption to get back up when knocked down. When you make recovery a habit, there is always hope. Even after striking out, your next at-bat could be a home run.

Failure, like gravity, gives us the necessary pressure to thrive. Without gravity, we wouldn't be able to function or accomplish the things that we use to build our identity. There would be no driving to work. There would be no nights out with friends. We'd be floating around with a very different anatomy. Gravity literally and figuratively keeps us grounded and makes all things on Earth possible. In that sense, gravity is essential. On the other hand, gravity is a major force exerting down on us and pushing against us. It compresses us and aims to squeeze us. Failure is like gravity. Failure pressures us. It pushes us down to keep us grounded, but it is also essential for us to live our lives.

---

* Jim Collins, "A Primer on the Warning Signs," JimCollins.com, May 2009, https://www.jimcollins.com/books/how-the-mighty-fall.html.

How do you ensure that you always get back up from failure, especially the cataclysmic failures that Collins spoke of? The answer partially goes back to something we talked about in the previous chapter: time, effort, and energy. But there is something else involved, and it relates to persistence. Combining these four concepts leads to a life-changing mantra: move your *tuches* (Yiddish word for "posterior").

MOVE YOUR *TUCHUS*

The phrase "Move your ass!" was emblazoned across Professor Marty Marshall's students' T-shirts that he once gave out. Standing in front of extremely intelligent Harvard Business School students, it was an unusual but careful wardrobe choice made to instill his philosophy for success in life and business. For Professor Marshall, there are certain intangibles that shape the world. One of my favorite mentors, his message to his students was clear: always give effort, time, and energy to what you're doing, and be persistent in that pursuit. Never stop moving. Move your tuches, always. Like a marathon, persistent, sustained effort leads to results. Most things in life are a marathon, not a sprint. Your enthusiasm in your pursuits should not be deterred because you *will* encounter failure. When you move your tuchus slowly and steadily through the marathon of life, you push your own boundaries and continue to grow. Sure, you may not have finished the marathon first, but challenging yourself to move your tuchus toward the finish line is itself a win.

Certainly, Marshall's point wasn't specific to just that class. In the business world, folks might sit on their laurels because of their focus on data. The numbers, forecasting, and risk mitigation can lead to a lack of innovation or action, and then it all collapses. Businesses need to keep moving to stay innovative. But the "Move your tuchus" principle applies to everything.

Professor Marshall understood a more profound truth about existence. His message is applicable to anybody pursuing their passions and goals. Once momentum ceases, it is difficult to get it started again. You have to keep moving forward, even if that means changing course along the way to account for happy accidents.

So-called failures are inevitable and are opportunities. You can either embrace failure or risk mediocrity. Be open to failure and the new directions these happy accidents take you. In other words, live life with *The Wonder Effect*. Recall that Dr. Keating's "loss" led to his greatest successes. On his way to becoming a home-run king, Babe Ruth first earned the moniker The King of Strikeouts.

Recovering from failure can be difficult. Experiencing an obstacle or a loss can throw us for a loop and knock us off our intended path. If that happens, how can you reorient yourself based on your multifaceted life? To answer that question, we can pull a useful theme from Lewis Carroll's *Alice in Wonderland*, which is that if you don't know where you're going, any road will take you there. The point is to fight inertia and move somewhere! Ideally, though, setting a compass to orient yourself toward your goal, destination, or intention helps you understand your personal criteria for success, helping you achieve what you set out to do.

CHAPTER 7

SET YOUR COMPASS

A person should set their goals as early as they can and devote all their energy and talent to getting there. With enough effort, they may achieve it. Or they may find something that is even more rewarding. But in the end, no matter the outcome, they will know they have been alive.

—WALT DISNEY

You now have the power to be wonder-minded. Up until now, previous chapters share a "You can do it, you just have to try" attitude. Now that you are not tethered by limiting beliefs, you may run into the problem of not knowing where you're going. To solve that issue and to sustain *The Wonder Effect* in your life, utilizing a life compass is a tool you can use to implement your newfound growth mindset in the right direction.

Why is going in the right direction important? During the height of the Soviet Union, many things were illegal that were basic rights elsewhere. For example, it was illegal to freely practice and express certain religious beliefs, including Judaism. At this time in Russia's history, an educator by the name of Rabbi Mendel Futerfas was arrested for teaching about Judaism and Jewish life to his fellow Jews in communist Russia. Imprisoned for fourteen years in a Siberian gulag, the rabbi witnessed mass destruction of inmate identity. His fellow inmates were otherwise very successful people who had cultivated lives of their own. But their constricted conditions robbed them of who they once were. The rabbi believed this was a purposeful tactic, as he saw how easy it was for the guards to break inmates down and control their behavior.

It became the goal of Rabbi Futerfas to, as much as he could, help others recover some semblance of themselves. He would ask fellow inmates about their former lives. One of those memorable stories included, of all things, his encounter with a former circus performer who specialized in the tightrope walk. Interested in the minutiae of the athleticism involved, Rabbi Futerfas inquired about the most difficult part of tightrope walking. The rabbi expected to hear about the difficulty to balance using the pole. Instead, the performer gave a surprising answer: the most difficult part was losing sight of the pole at the end of the tightrope. When you don't have direction, focusing on balance and walking is reduced, making the process to turn around or find safety dangerous. The most difficult part is not seeing or having direction.

For years afterward, the rabbi used this story to make a simple argument: if you want to stay balanced as you grow and learn, you need to move forward with intentionality and with a clear vision of where your next step can take you. You can explore your interests with an adventurous spirit. You can get up and press on in the face of failure. These are crucial components to success, but you also need to know what direction you're facing as you continue to make strides forward. This requires setting and following a life compass.

YOUR LIFE COMPASS

A life compass is about making decisions aligned with your visions, ambitions, and interests. The purpose of this life compass is to lead you where you want to go. There's chosen destinations, and there's where you are now. You have the map, so to speak. To dictate your direction, you need a life compass to help you travel effectively to your destinations. That means being thoughtful and considerate about how you travel toward your crystallized goals. That doesn't mean you can't continue to experiment, but by this stage you should have a clearer interest to generate real expertise. With a life compass, you can harness your earlier sense of adventure in a way that is not destructive or ambling but focused on energy that leads to the results you want. Like a flight that is always course correcting, you will land where you need to go.

How do you know which direction to go? How do you set your life compass? The points of a life compass are determined by four things: values, priorities, principles, and ambitions. They help set the direction like north, south, east, and west. Unconsciously or consciously, you make choices to follow those four points. You've probably heard the phrase "moral compass," which guides us to act with a specific morality based on our beliefs of right and wrong. A life compass works similarly, but it extends beyond morality and includes all action in the direction of your life's dreams, goals, and interests. Next is determining how to use your life compass as a tool to guide you on the path of your journey.

To give an example, let's say your life compass is set with these four points (values, priorities, principles, and ambitions). There are multiple coordinates on your map that have destinations that include meeting financial priorities and family values. Now imagine that you have been making the choice to spend a hundred hours a week pursuing financial priorities. Clearly, the family values will suffer. Using your life compass, redirect yourself back to your family to remain balanced in finding your targeted destinations. If you set a value of spending 50 percent of your time with your family, that means you need to adjust how you use your life compass, spending less time pursuing financial priorities and more time with family.

SET YOUR COMPASS

As a tool, the life compass provides direction to get to your destinations. Setting your life compass means not proceeding with abandon but reflecting thoughtfully on your priorities, values, principles, and ambitions to determine appropriate life coordinates. It helps you determine if you are pursuing one path more than another. If you set a priority to make one million dollars and are willing to do anything to achieve that goal (cheat, kill, etc.), you've set one destination but failed to balance it with a moral, value-based cardinal direction.

Remember to always be thoughtful. I have a friend living in Texas who is the epitome of a life compass that helps him change direction intentionally to live a more balanced life. Family and finances are cardinal points on his compass. He wants to become a lawyer to produce a salary that will take care of his family's needs. Accepted into Yale Law School, his family didn't want to uproot from Texas. Navigating with his life compass, and after consulting with his family, he was able to fly to Connecticut to study at Yale for three days a week, then fly back for the rest of the week to be with his family. By taking this multi-coordinate path guided by his life compass, his intentional journey fulfills his life's priorities, values, principles, and ambitions.

You will need to identify any conflicting values in your destination. Work and family, for example, are often conflicting values. When these points are in conflict, with one pulling you in a certain direction only for the other to take you in the exact opposite direction, you will need to use your life compass to determine the most appropriate path that gets you to multiple destinations.

Explorers often change direction based on the current of the sea or the mountains blocking their path. With their trusty compass, they are ensured to maneuver through difficult obstacles while staying on the intended path. You may veer off course, but the general direction and destination remain the same when you use a life compass to stay aligned.

Don't forget that you can do whatever you put your mind to do. Don't stereotype yourself negatively. At the moment, you may not be a fantastic musician or chef. That doesn't mean you cannot apply yourself to acquire expertise in either of those subjects. Don't let that limited thinking discussed earlier prevent you from giving yourself a coordinate to find with your life compass. It's only through action that you can become your ideal self.

ACT TO BECOME

The time people spend planning often heavily outweighs the time they spend executing the plan. This makes sense because folks often want to put their best foot forward. But there is a troubling consequence to this practice: acting becomes inferior to the importance of thought and planning. Studying for the test seems to take ten times as long as taking the test itself. Emphasizing a plan or thought instead of balancing it with action creates its own obstacles. Because there are no limits to the thoughts you can think, you can think until the ability to take action passes.

When it comes to experience, the merger of thought and actions (rather than knowledge acquisition) generates experience. And people tend to favor those with a lot of experience. I personally value those with experience far more than experts. Experts trend toward the theoretical; those with experience balance theory and action to create a better understanding of how reality and theory confront each other.

Being balanced in this manner will benefit from your life compass. With each new experience, your map could add or change coordinated destinations (your goals). Keeping fast to your life compass and staying mindful of your priorities, values, principles, and ambitions will ensure you are oriented toward alignment as your journey changes.

Paralysis by analysis is real, and if you believe you can think your way into a different type of behavior, you are sorely mistaken. Thought is circular. Ideas often feel new or fresh when in fact you don't realize that they are old ideas redressed with modern words. With overthinking, you are back where you started and going nowhere fast. Conversely, action begets change and growth in how you think about the world and act within it. In my estimation, then, action should be emphasized. If you wanted to be a great athlete, you could read as many books as you could lay your eyes on. But if you are just reading, then you are not practicing the sport associated with your field of athleticism. You just can't get it until you do it.

The unbalanced dichotomy between planning and acting should be integrated and balanced. The learning and planning process must take place while acting—just as it did with Harold and his purple crayon. When you place more emphasis on action, you can act yourself into a different person or mode of thinking. You can will the new version of yourself into existence.

The idea of using a compass to transition from imperfection to something closer to perfection might sound abstract. Here's an experience of my own to illustrate the concept. Years ago, I felt the pressures of hiring a staff for the first time, around when I started my first business. I had never conducted hiring interviews before. Who was I to pretend like I knew how to interview well? Because my compass was giving me direction to run this business, I embraced that it would be an imperfect process. My new identity was to be the leader, so I had to act myself into that identity. No amount of thinking or planning would make me the leader. Devising a strategy, philosophy, and goals for the interviews, I gave myself the leeway to accept that I may be a little sloppy in the execution. And I was sloppy. But the experience taught me how to adjust and get better. Because I was acting like the leader, I became the leader. Or, as many agree, fake it till you make it.

SET YOUR COMPASS

The process of acting our way into being echoes sentiments of bestselling author and teacher Don Miguel Ruiz. Situated within his book *The Four Agreements*, Ruiz argues that there is a clear process to acting one's way into being. When acting for the first time, you gain confidence. As you move forward with confidence, you learn to trust yourself and gain the trust of others. When you act with trust, you gain faith and believe in your capacity to be an expert.* From imperfection to faith, incremental baby steps of working through flaws become a method to act your way into a new form of thinking and being. Along the way, your compass will keep you steadfastly oriented toward your end goal despite the imperfections that crop up.

Ruiz's ideas are not dissimilar to the James–Lange theory of emotions, which suggests that bodily changes come before emotional or intellectual changes. William James and Carl Lange surmised that making oneself smile leads to one becoming happier, and not the other way around. Over a hundred years later, modern research proved both men to be absolutely correct. The mere act of smiling releases neuropeptides, dopamine, serotonin, and endorphins that reduce stress, depression, and anxiety.† Smiling isn't necessarily a

---

* Don Miguel Ruiz, *The Four Agreements: A Practical Guide to Personal Freedom* (San Rafael, CA: Amber-Allen, 1997), 14–33.

† Ronald E. Riggio, "There's Magic in Your Smile," *Psychology Today*, June 25, 2012, https://www.psychologytoday.com/us/blog/cutting-edge-leadership/201206/there-s-magic-in-your-smile.

response to happiness; rather, it is a catalyst to manifest happiness. Acting occurs before being. Review your compass, redirect your path, and begin acting your way into a new mode of thinking and behaving. When you realize that something as small as a smile can have a profound effect on you, you can then understand that large consequences result from a series of smaller actions.

THE MICRO DONE GETS THE MACRO DONE

"The micro done gets the macro done" is one of my favorite motivational concepts. The cliché translation of this phrase might be that a thousand-mile journey begins with the first step. Layering on the micro actions will, eventually, ensure that the macro action is completed.

South African leader Desmond Tutu once remarked that there was only one way to eat an elephant: "a bite at a time."* He meant that people often put these very large and superficially insurmountable goals and dreams in their imagined future. Tutu reminds us that a lot of micro actions, in the aggregate, add up to the big ambition getting accomplished. How one gets started has no particular right answer. You reach your goal by taking the journey one step at a time. Start

---

* Denise Fournier, "The Only Way to Eat an Elephant," *Psychology Today*, April 24, 2018, https://www.psychologytoday.com/us/blog/mindfully-present-fully-alive/201804/the-only-way-eat-elephant.

in any way possible, even if that's with taking the smallest bite on your plate first.

If you have a direction but get stuck on where to start, solicit assistance from one with experience. This is a very effective micro action that can lead to further micro actions. Asking for help from others can accelerate your successes enormously despite the general feeling that you shouldn't be doing it. Asking for help is associated with societal myths about failure: simply asking for it somehow signals your weaknesses and need for somebody else. But on the other hand, having somebody help you is often the precise assistance you need to maintain your path toward your ambitions.

Don't confuse asking for help with seeking mentorship, as I talked about in an earlier chapter. Mentors provide deep, meaningful, and communal relationships. Asking for help, on the other hand, is generating a quick leg up in a time of need. It is not required that helpers help in a face-to-face sense. Whether that means from books, blogs, or other forms of media where they have archived their thoughts, solicit advice and guidance from those experts (foxes) that offer. Choosing the correct people from without aligns with getting the micro done. In the cardinal direction on your life's compass, you are going to know somebody who is also interested in those same pursuits. Be vulnerable enough to start asking for help from those people. It is really that simple.

I have found this to be personally true in almost every instance: people like helping other people. Sure, you will be rejected by some. I can remember when I first pursued my interests in real estate. I literally emailed everybody I could think of who had ever articulated knowledge or expertise in the subject. Some of them completely ignored me. Some responded. And some were willing to sit down with me and work out everything they had learned in a conversational manner. A helper's advice guided me through my first investment opportunity. The micro effort of acquiring help from without was a game changer for me. Over the years, I've continued to use the micro to get the macro done.

Reaching out to others for help is so effective that you will occasionally forget the titanic impact they had in launching you into your successes. Do your best to keep that perspective by advising others at that same level of guidance you received. *Pay it forward*, in other words. Doing so will keep you moving forward as well, as we will discuss in more detail in the next chapter. Asking for outside help is an *action* that can help you behave into a new way of thinking. Because doing means you are learning. And learning means you are moving forward.

DOING IS LEARNING

Have you ever watched a 3D printer create something right before your eyes? If not, I'd encourage you to look it up, as it is quite remarkable. You'll see that the printer does not plop out the thing it's printing all at once. It builds microscopic layers upon microscopic layers of plastic or metal "ink," moving back and forth meticulously. At first, the printed object is a few droplets of hardening material. After several layers, the object's shape faintly emerges.

Like the James–Lange theory, like Ruiz's concept of acquiring faith in yourself, and like my notion of embracing imperfection on the way to perfection, a 3D printed object requires a repeated process of smaller events and actions that lead to the emergence of the overall picture. In order to grow and learn, you must layer yourself with actions.

The more you put yourself into action, the more your body and mind lets the training kick in. It reminds me of my foray into running a marathon. I wasn't exactly a runner, and I knew the difficulties that running a marathon entailed, so I endeavored to train in the months leading up to the event. Putting myself into action, the running part of my training got my mind prepared for what was to come. When that starting gun went off and I took off, my shin splints fired up. A terror shot up my spine. *Oh, wow! How am I going to finish this? I have twenty-six more miles to go.* It was a daunting feeling. But thanks to the action involved in my training, running and not stopping was ingrained in my body. As Lawrence Taylor used to say, "It's mind over matter. If you don't mind, it doesn't matter." So I decided that I didn't need to strategize or focus on alleviating my pain. I let my mental training kick in and direct me where to go. By acting yourself into existence through the micro actions of self-training, you hijack yourself to get something grand accomplished. To get started, you need to lower the barrier for entry.

PACK YOUR BAGS IF YOU WANT TO GET MOTIVATED

You can lead yourself into new behaviors by first starting with adjacent actions. What does that mean? Take getting healthy, for example, by joining a gym. An insignificant percentage of folks actually use their gym membership after the initial purchase. Generating the necessary motivation for action isn't simply purchasing the membership; you need to examine the *reasons* you want to get healthier and work backward from there.

There could be all sorts of reasons you have for getting healthy. But reason alone won't motivate. Motivation comes from what the reason means to you. Maybe it's to ensure spryness and longevity enough to dance at your grandchild's wedding. Maybe it's to maximize your daily energy to complete other tasks. Or maybe getting healthy would allow your return to your favorite but neglected recreational activities. Conviction or meaning will motivate behavior. Some people might prefer eating ice cream to living longer.

Let's say there's a person who wants to get healthy for recreation. Specifically, they want to rejoin their recreational soccer team. But perhaps they're worried they'll be a liability to their team, so they bought a gym membership but never

SET YOUR COMPASS

go to the gym. The problem is, of course, going to the gym doesn't fulfill the *meaning* they receive from playing. Being with their friends is the meaning. My advice to this person would be to go play soccer while they are out of shape. They'll be heaving and wheezing and panting and puffing around their friends, and that will generate all of the motivation they need to get healthy fast. They'll feel highly motivated to hit the gym to lessen that tiring experience for the next game. The *meaning* of wanting to be in shape—playing soccer with friends—will be an effective motivator. Our perceptions of cause and effect are often inverted.

The effect often creates the cause and not the other way around. Another common place this happens in people's lives is when they vacation. Too many are workaholics who always put off that next trip as they continue to toil away. Instead, they need to pack their bags to get motivated. With the bag packed, they should then buy a ticket and proclaim publicly they are going on vacation. They can deal with the details along the way. The proverbial packed bag will be a daily reminder of the *reason* they need to go on vacation—to take a relaxing break. When their belongings are stuffed in the suitcase, tickets purchased, and they've publicly committed, there is very little recourse other than to go to the airport and travel to where those bags intend to go. There is a need to overcommit in order to commit.

Be it soccer or travel or anything on your life's compass, hijack yourself into behaving in such a way that forces you to live up to your commitments. If you commit to the soccer team you had been waiting to join in the shared text thread, you have hijacked yourself by stating publicly to your community of soccer friends that you will be getting in shape. When that happens, there is a higher likelihood that you'll follow through and induce or influence yourself to move toward the ambitions of your compass.

WALK THE TIGHTROPE

When navigating with your life's compass, you will find that too much of *this* or *that* will throw you off balance. Being lost is a natural part of the journey. The tightrope walk to success means knowing where you are going. In moments that you become lost or cannot see where your steps are taking you, redirect using the points of your compass. In his last lecture, Professor Randy Pausch, who was diagnosed with a terminal disease, famously said, "If you lead your life the right way, the rest will take care of itself. The dreams will come to you."* Use your compass to lead your life in the right direction.

Personal growth is a destination, and in order to arrive you need to develop the correct directional tools. Keeping that destination in mind or reevaluating how you may navigate

---

* Randy Pausch, *The Last Lecture: Lessons in Living* (London: Hodder, 2010), 132.

SET YOUR COMPASS

toward that destination when you are lost is essential to arriving and thriving. Further, sojourned destinations while on the longer path to the bigger destination will help you arrive with expertise. When you act toward smaller goals aligned with your larger ambitions, the big picture naturally comes into focus. The micro done gets the macro done. In his second year in the league, NFL quarterback Russell Wilson used a playoff loss to set a new life-compassed direction: win the Super Bowl. Immediately after the loss, as if using the adjacent compass points for stop-offs on the way to building elite expertise at his position, he gave himself smaller goals. They included winning the division, throwing for four thousand yards in a season, winning league MVP, and others. In his mind, if he focused on accomplishing these smaller goals, they would lead him toward his biggest ambition. In 2014, the Wilson-led Seattle Seahawks won the Super Bowl.

Set your directional points with smaller goals that are along the path of your cardinal direction. These micro steps lead to the macro output, which then assists the achievement of the ambitious thing you once thought impossible. With continued movement and momentum, a compass allows you to explore your interests, passions, and calling.

Generating a clear vision of the direction you're heading is crucial to success. Visualize your future. Or write out a fictionalized version of your future life. Your hand guiding the words will be the first action you take in a long journey to accomplishing that future. You are the architect of your future, and it would benefit you to render and model the structure you want your life to be.

You will come into contact with the various communities built around your interests and ambitions. When you have those communal connections, your relationships with mentors and your eventual role as a mentor will help keep you grounded and focused on your next destination and opportunities for growth. Mentors can seem excessively domineering and overly successful from afar, but you will come to find that they are real people—a lot like you. That is grounding. People want to see you succeed, and they may connect you with the paths that accelerate your arrival. Leverage your role models and then become a role model yourself. Live to serve others because so many others have served you.

CHAPTER 8

SERVE OTHERS

When you see what needs to be fixed, and how to fix it, then you have found a piece of the world that G-d has left for you to complete.

—LUBAVITCHER REBBE

There are many things in this world that were here before you, and you didn't do anything to help them come into being or to support the people who created them. Preceding generations provided those advantages. Therefore, it's time to pay it forward. When you are grounded with this perspective, you can see the importance of serving others, not just for their sake but for yours too.

This lesson is taught in the Talmudic story of Honi HaMe'agel. Honi comes upon a man planting a carob tree that won't bear fruit for seventy years. Honi asks him if he believes he will live another seventy years to see the fruit of the tree. The man replies, "When I was born into this world, I found many beautiful carob trees planted by those who came before me. Just as my ancestors planted trees for me, I am planting trees for my children and grandchildren." In a similar vein as Rip Van Winkle (but written two thousand years earlier), and after sleeping for seventy years, Honi wakes to find the man's children nourished by the tree, invigorated with an opportunity to thrive. The moral of the story is that by planting the tree, the man gave future generations the ability to succeed just as was provided to him.

Too often, people live their lives without the perspective Honi received. In order to become grounded like Honi, you need only the simple recognition and commonsense wisdom that you didn't accomplish everything by yourself. Your life would not be where it is if not for several other people helping you along the way. Others are instrumental in our success. If you've been following the advice of this book, you've sought out mentors who are successful achievers. For many, including Hal Elrod, part of becoming a success means having their successful habits inculcated within us. When you cultivate an awareness of the many people who catapulted you to success, it becomes so obvious that affording those opportunities to others is an essential part of giving back. Additionally, it is essential to continuing our own growth.

PLANT TREES

After my oldest son finished school, he and one of his friends decided to briefly move into my home to develop business ideas. Because of the business efforts I had made for myself, I was in a position to give them my time and help them generate ideas. What they learned very quickly is what many of us learn when we set out on the path toward ambitions: obstacles immediately rear their heads.

My main role was to help them conceptualize ways of creating the things they came up with and remove obstacles while pursuing their interests. Just as one specific example, as their business plan started crystalizing, it became clear that they needed to start an LLC. Faced with that task, what should they do next? Should they contact a lawyer? Should they use a website service that helps users form LLCs? Do they even know of their options in creating one? My role was to educate them on their options to remove the obstacle of not knowing, but also to prevent analysis paralysis.

Their business ideas might not have sold one widget or could have sold a million. Once they started seeing the possibilities, they understood they needed to lay the groundwork for what the business could become. Helping them remove the barriers that stand between an idea and a functioning business, I could see their eyes open up with wonder. *The Wonder Effect* of optimistic curiosity sparked in them a greater imaginative pursuit of their possibilities. They were like kids in a sandbox with complete autonomy to shape a sandcastle to their liking. They learned that once you pursue something, obstacles are just tools for growth. At a certain point in my life, I learned those same lessons and was happy to help plant that seed of growth for them. In their own garden, they now can grow, stretch, and continue to branch out. Eventually, they will help others plant their own trees. Helping others to an extent that it causes or requires a sacrifice—such as taking the time to engage—is actually a luxury. And there's a certain joy in being able to see and proliferate another's journey toward success without any intent to benefit.

As mentioned in the introduction, the Hebrew word *ma'aser*—to give charity—is related to the world *wealthy*. This suggests that we become enriched when we spend time enriching others. We perform a new role, we get to know ourselves in a new way, we continue to grow, *and* we help others on that journey for themselves.

We have the power to influence those seeking our advice. The ability to serve others is humanity's superpower. And with great power comes great responsibility, as Spider-Man would say. Superheroes—the Supermans, the Spider-Mans, and all the rest—aren't in it for money or glory. It's always the supervillain whose plan is a self-serving search for enrichment and empowerment. Don't be a jerk; instead, use your superpower like a superhero. Your unique capacities can benefit others and contribute positive impacts on the world.

SERVE OTHERS

Recognize that those starting out on their journeys are living in a somewhat scary and uncertain time of their life. They are unseasoned in their new endeavors. Trying to see through fog, it is not always easy to generate clarity on the direction to take. For example, when I was starting out, I did not have any sort of safety net, guidance, or methods to discover myself. Despite having a few regrets, I count myself lucky for experiences that quilted *The Wonder Effect* into my life. Without those few planted trees, who knows where I'd be. Because not having mentors is more common than otherwise, it is imperative that you continue to plant the trees of guidance for those who ask.

Because communities are built on individuals helping one another, every person's success is heavily reliant on the kindnesses of others. When you start out in a community, you are uplifted by others and launched toward your successes. After a while, you become established and successful. Around that time, newcomers enter. To help the entire community thrive, it becomes your responsibility to help guide those newcomers, just as others had done before with you. Coming full circle and giving back to the community means fulfilling your part in the overall social contract.

Your parents or mentors took care of you, and if you didn't fulfill your part of the social contract, it would be like not taking care of your own children or the children in your community. You would be taking the fruit of the tree without using the seeds to plant one for future generations. In a very real way, not giving back disrupts and ruins the cycle of life. The community will eventually die.

CIRCLE BACK

Viktor Frankl's book *Man's Search for Meaning* shares his experiences in a Nazi concentration camp. In it, he argues that how you envision your future affects your ability to thrive; he says you must find meaning and purpose.* Helping others when they need help automatically imbues your life with meaning because you, perhaps unknowingly, joined a community. Being part of something larger puts a stop to the belief that your existence is a closed loop that begins and ends with you.

Even in the face of his beliefs about purpose, Frankl had his doubts. After he started work on his now-iconic book, and after he survived Nazi concentration camps, he was one of the lone dissenters of Freudian theories. That isolated him from his own community. He felt drained and thought that maybe his work wouldn't be fruitful. Then he received a visit from a stranger, a traveler who had a message for him from the Lubavitcher Rebbe: "Please send Dr. Frankl my regards. And pass the following message on to him: that I said that he should be strong and continue his work with complete

---

* Viktor E Frankl, *Man's Search for Meaning* (Boston: Beacon Press, 2006), 35–40.

SERVE OTHERS

resolve. No matter what, he should not give up. If he remains strong and committed, he will certainly prevail." Frankl felt freshly inspired and reinvigorated with purpose. He then continued and finished his book.

What Frankl has done since this is pretty well-known. His message has had a profound impact on the academic community and has helped millions of people. Even the most seemingly self-assured person carries doubts. If not for the encouragement of others, we can lose sight of our purpose.

With a purpose, you are intimately and deeply connected with those around you like interwoven roots below the surface of a forest. Helping others creates a circularity that sustains both your purpose and your function within the community. When you help others in this manner, you will perpetuate the positivity given to you by your mentors into the next generation.

You bring a unique life quilt to the community. By leading with your unique circumstances, you will benefit the community like open-system economics of specialization. In a closed system, you have to do it all; in an open system, you can do what you do best. For example, if a grocery store wanted to stock as many cucumbers and tomatoes as possible and went to two farmers to cultivate their crops, each might say they could produce two hundred of each, generating four hundred total vegetables.

In an open system, however, the farmers are allowed to specialize. One may have soil better suited to cucumbers while the other a better sprinkler system to grow tomatoes. When they specialize on their strengths, they can each yield seven hundred of their selected crop, filling the grocery store with 1,400 vegetables to provide for their hungry customers. In short, specialization is a strength, and yours will be aided by the specialization of others within a community to ensure the hungry minds of the future have all of the tools they need to succeed.

When you contribute your unique insights as a mentor, you will be doing more than simply passing on what your mentors taught you. You will also be adding your unique knowledge to the communal whole. And the possibility of adding new wisdom and knowledge to the community creates the motivation to continue adventuring for more.

FIND SUCCESS THE RIGHT WAY

Eventually, we all must face the hard reality of the limitations of our longevity. We are finite beings that, one day, will die. Your time is your most precious commodity, and your effort is your second. To fulfill a life purpose through communal contribution, come to understand the simple fact that you don't know the true limit of your time. You could die at any moment, even today, and that truth should motivate you into action. It sounds morbid, but this might be your last day to give back or to travel toward your ambitions. Our physical

SERVE OTHERS

death is, at any given moment, entirely possible. Make the most of the time you are given.

Now, I'm not saying that you should immediately book a flight to Vegas to bet everything you have on red. I'm saying you need to sober yourself to the nature of time. It is your most important resource; spend that resource carefully. You may find that reframing your sense of time gives you a new direction. Grounding yourself through this humbling perspective may act as the catalyst to give back to your community. If you are here for a reason, why waste a second on anything other than fulfilling that purpose?

You know you are going about success the correct way if you imagine it as a carrot dangling on a stick and always slightly out of your reach rather than a carrot that you eat to satisfy your hunger. Once you achieve something, keep pushing the bar of success beyond its previous point in order to continue achieving. Proper success requires recognizing the limitlessness of your growth potential.

ACCEPT YOUR LIFE AS A MIRACLE

Another humbling way to come to terms with your life, to get grounded, and give back is to acknowledge that, sometimes, our successes have nothing to do with us whatsoever. In fact, if it wasn't for Stanislav Petrov, none of us might be here enjoying a book at this very moment. During the Cold War, on September 26, 1983, the Soviet Union's early warning nuclear attack detection system indicated that a total of five missiles, one initial missile and four trailing missiles, had launched from the United States and were set to destroy major Soviet cities.

On that day and at that particular hour, Petrov was commanding the early warning system. Protocol dictated that Petrov immediately inform specific colleagues to begin retaliatory missile strikes on American targets. Suspicious of the system's accuracy, Petrov decided to wait for corroborating evidence beyond what the computer was telling him. Shockingly, he decided to wait until after the supposed bombs were to detonate to see if, indeed, the nuclear missiles had been launched. When no bomb detonated, he decided that the four remaining must also have been errors. He was correct.

Each country's arsenal of nuclear weapons was in the hundreds. Had Petrov decided to notify the chain of command, it would have launched a tit-for-tat five missiles back immediately. The United States would have then launched five in retaliation, leading to five more from the USSR, and continuing that trend until complete nuclear annihilation of the earth ensued. That day, Petrov's decision helped the world avoid the apocalypse. Nearly twenty years after the release of the darkly funny film about a nuclear holocaust, *Dr. Strangelove or: How I Learned to Stop Worrying and Love the Bomb*, the world had unknowingly experienced in real life a situation that had only existed in film and the fever dreams of the paranoid. From just this one historical incident, we can clearly see that we are lucky to even be alive. Now, compound the many other things that have led you to your current moment. You are a walking miracle.

The story about Stanislav Petrov is an example of all of humanity experiencing a miracle. But the truth is that each of us is built from a multitude of unseen and tiny miracles every day. So, what's the probability of your being born? One in 400 trillion!* It's the probability of 2.5 million people getting together—about the population of San Diego—each to play a game of dice with *trillion-sided dice*. They each roll the dice and come up with the exact same number—say, 550,343,279,001. A miracle is an event so unlikely as to be almost impossible. By that definition, I've just proven that you are a miracle. Now go forth and feel and act like the miracle that you are.

Although we are too busy in our daily lives to give them much reflection, we cannot take them for granted.

Your life is a miracle, and you can use the lessons learned to set new goals as a mentor. When you look at the difference between where you started your life and where you are now, that is a huge difference that can act as inspiration for both

---

* Dr. Ali Binazir, "Are You a Miracle? On the Probability of You Being Born," Huffpost, June 16, 2011, https://www.huffpost.com/entry/probability-being-born_b_877853.

you and those aspiring to travel on their own journeys. Share your life miracles with others, and help them see their own life as a miracle worth cultivating.

IF YOU'VE BEEN BLESSED, BE A BLESSING

Becoming aware of the communal circumstances that have provided you with all of your life's blessings gives you reason to lead with gratitude. Being grateful is the fertile ground from which meaningful contribution sprouts. Experiencing gratitude clarifies the substantial contribution of every little blessing to our happiness and success.

Gratitude does not mean becoming so satisfied that you no longer have the motivation to act. Instead, gratitude creates the optimal attitude to become your best self as a mentor and member of the community. For as the adage goes, it's not your aptitude but your attitude that determines your altitude.

Attitude = Disposition: If your attitude is positive, then in most situations you will see the better side of things. And opportunities for good can emerge. Even when something that you don't want to occur happens, your mind will problem-solve in a way that becomes self-fulfilling toward the good and positive. Aptitude = Intelligence: This is something that is neutral. Even though it is about understanding, it requires direction. So, if you are disposed to a negative attitude, then that directs your intelligence to answer the negative thought, *Why*

SERVE OTHERS

do these things always happen to me? and your intelligence will respond. The opposite is also true.

Shaping your attitude with gratitude to be a blessing for the community occurs through intrinsic, rather than extrinsic, rewards. To clarify the two types of rewards, an extrinsic reward is something that you are given as a result of doing something. If you tell your child you will buy them ice cream if they clean up their room, the extrinsic reward functions as a payment or incentive for them to complete the desired task. The ice cream is not inherently related to the task. Alternatively, an intrinsic reward is if you clean up your room on your own in order to benefit either from the organization (accessing things more efficiently) or emotionally (feeling pride in accomplishing the task). In the case of intrinsic rewards, the biggest rewards are the opportunity and consequences, which are connected to the task rather than the task itself.

Those motivated to clean up their rooms to acquire ice cream are fundamentally misunderstanding the purpose of taking action in a particular direction. Since the reward and opportunity are not related, extrinsic rewards actually prevent growth by pulling the actor in two different directions. In the short term, extrinsic motivators may seem to have a positive effect on somebody, but it won't last long. Further, those seeking rewards misaligned with their deeds are more likely to become self-serving people who don't see how their actions affect others, positively or negatively.

Intrinsic rewards, on the other hand, create a sense of having fewer limitations and belonging to an interconnected world. *Now that the room is clean,* the wonder-minded person will think, *I have many more opportunities in front of me.* Intrinsic rewards peel away the layers of obstacles on the path toward ambition. They create long-term values and a nuanced understanding of the connectedness of everything. They will understand that their actions have consequences, ensuring that they dial their compass with a sense of purpose directed at communal contribution.

When you develop your abilities as a mentor, it will be to the greater benefit of your mentee and the community in general if you guide others with intrinsic rewards rather than extrinsic. Why? Because the former creates a sense of self-motivation and self-reliance. It offers a greater hope that the individual who learns the value of intrinsic motivation will plant their own proverbial carob tree for the next cycle of mentees.

YOUR BEST SELF BECOMES THEIR BEST SELF

Serving others without directly benefiting yourself is one of the most altruistic things you could possibly do. You may experience joy in mentoring, but that is hardly the driving force behind serving others. Seeing others succeed typically drives this behavior. And when serving others becomes part of your identity, that's you at your best self.

SERVE OTHERS

To guide somebody in that altruistic way causes the life lessons that have entered your heart to enter the heart of others. Your best self has, to some degree, been instilled in another to allow that person to unlock and define their own best self. When you uplift just a single person with the insights of your successes, imagine the tapestry of mentors around the world helping the next up-and-comers realize that the world believes in them. They, then, begin to believe that their time and effort is worth it because mentors have given them their time and effort. When somebody gives that to us, we can feel our capacity opening up and begin to believe in ourselves: *I'm meaningful. I can achieve. I can create. I can do anything.*

We are responsible for keeping the snowball of *The Wonder Effect* rolling into an avalanche so that it can continue a cycle of hope, optimism, curiosity, and success. When you start out, your dream can become your passion. As your passions are realized, you can teach the process to others, and your service to the community becomes your new passion and purpose.

Many people cannot see the true possibilities in their future. Perhaps very recently, you were one of those people. As you continue your journey toward fulfilling your dreams, ambitions, and goals, don't forget to instill what you've learned in others. The curiosity, imagination, creativity, openness, and courage of *The Wonder Effect* will help the impossible become possible.

CONCLUSION

If you want a different life, you have to become a different person.

—DR. BENJAMIN HARDY

As you near the end, I encourage you to wonder on and continue your adventures.

At the time of writing, I'm working on one of the bigger real estate deals of my life. The owner wants to close the purchase quickly. Acquiring the money from my investors and completing the due diligence must be expedited. Making it more difficult, the purchase is out of state, and there are many small state laws that could change how I would otherwise evaluate the investment.

The money for this deal was put up yesterday. The contract has been signed. And all of a sudden, I feel a little freaked out. There is a gnawing feeling that some detail has been overlooked. Am I making a big mistake? Because of my fiduciary responsibility to my investors' money, it adds quite a bit of pressure. My emotional stress is exacerbated by that creeping feeling of false idols or false experts swimming back into my system. Am I an imposter? Am I expert enough to handle this? But I know myself, and I created my curriculum by doing the underwriting properly. My life's quilt and curriculum gave me the confidence and assurance that I know what I'm doing. In the run-up, I've explored by checking all of the numbers again and again. I've adventurously reorganized the data to see what new information I can glean. This is real estate, after all, so I've embraced the fact that it could fail for any reason. And I've pressed on by asking the right questions. Did I make sure the property zoning issues were resolved? Check. Did I apply for the multifamily license? I did. Is there enough parking? Yes. By the time this goes to print, I will have signed all of the paperwork.

This job has created an illuminating moment for me. I intellectually understand the components of *The Wonder Effect*. But even then, I still feel the anxieties, fears, and other obstacles that often get in the way of our thoughtful pursuits. This just goes to show that we never fully arrive at a destination. We are always on the journey, and we always need to work hard to keep moving forward. Am I ready for this investment? Not fully, no. But I do have the experience

CONCLUSION

and expertise to keep myself moving forward as it plays itself out. I wield a purple crayon that can, at any moment, help me find the solutions to the problems that present themselves.

While pursuing your ambitions, every component of *The Wonder Effect* is crucial to maximizing your potential to achieve your dreams. These are not prescriptive steps but essential and core concepts. Each core idea helps you continue forward, especially when you stub your toe along the way. When you fill your life with *The Wonder Effect*, you will always be moving in the right direction. As the Chinese proverb says, the thousand-mile walk begins with one step.

STAY ALOFT

In aviation, there is a specific type of being lost—of sensory loss—that inevitably ends in death. It's called a graveyard spiral, but in popular culture it's better known as a death spiral. This phenomenon occurs when a pilot no longer knows which direction they are headed. Imagine flying over the ocean where the sea and sky look the same. When entering the spiral, the pilot's inner ear prevents them from sensing up from down. Therefore, the pilot can no longer discern the plane's positioning. Death spirals and steady flying feel the same. The horrific reality is that pilots in a death spiral will hit the ocean completely unaware they were about to meet their demise. In a very literal sense, these pilots have lost their compass. They are unaware of where to go, how to fix the issue, or that there's even an issue.

You'll be glad to know that, over the years, aviators have developed training methods to escape a graveyard spin after entry. This training focuses on unique readings of instrumentation and manipulating the plane to put them back on the proper course. By way of analogy, you now have a life compass to act as your navigating instrumentation. If you enter our proverbial death spiral, you can use the instrumentations of *The Wonder Effect* to ensure you maintain your altitude.

So, while I felt a sense of anxiety and fear that my aforementioned real estate deal had some overlooked flaw and that I had accidentally entered a death spiral, I kept checking my instruments. They pointed me in the right direction to put myself and my investors on a path forward.

But it's not just a path forward that helps us achieve our goals and ambitions. As Dr. Benjamin Hardy, organizational psychologist, says, "If you want a different life, you must become a different person."* The Wright brothers, whom I talked about briefly, illustrate Dr. Hardy's proposition. With a disposition toward action that transformed them from bicycle manufacturers into the forebears of flight, they had no degrees in aviation. They didn't even have high school

---

* Benjamin Hardy, *Willpower Doesn't Work: Discover the Hidden Keys to Success* (New York: Hachette Books, 2018), 54.

CONCLUSION

diplomas. Nobody considered them official experts in any way. Yet they continued to pursue the ambitions and dreams they ended up fulfilling despite their lack of diplomas and acceptance among their peers. On his way to expertise, Orville Wright, for example, ran his own printing business and weekly newspaper at fifteen years of age. By the time they made their aviation accomplishments, they beat out the United States government, who had enlisted an army of experts to develop modern aircraft. (Although there was no way anyone could have known, it turned out that developing new air technologies would prove extremely important in turning the tide of World War I.)

At Kitty Hawk, North Carolina, the site of their famous 1903 first flight, they experienced over a dozen major crashes. But they were not concerned with their micro failures along the way. They ended up putting themselves out there with a disposition to action. They used the information gleaned from the "failure" of crashes to proceed forward. Taking comfort in forward progress, the obvious value of the bruises, scars, and experiences of their failures was that they propelled their successes.

The Wright brothers, echoing Reid Hoffman, seemed to jump off the aviation cliff and built their plane on the way down. The crashes stemming from their penchant for action and experience far outweighed what could have been gained from intellectual understanding alone. Like the Wright brothers, you must manifest yourself through your actions, even if that means needing to first crush false idols and get to know yourself again.

BEGIN AGAIN

Just recently, I had an opportunity to guide my son using the tools in this book. In this particular instance, I was mentoring him on how to get to know himself again. My goal was to encourage a wondrous mind and jumpstart his journey toward his ambitions. During our conversation, I posed the thought experiment about an ideal future where money was no issue. What would he want to pursue? I threw out some brainstorming ideas like returning to school, learning independently about something, throwing himself at a specific experience. What would he want to do?

To my delighted surprise, his reaction to me was, "I love this question." And then he started exploring all of these possibilities out loud. By the end of our talk, it wasn't clear if he was any closer to knowing the answer. But it was clear that talking it out gave him a disposition toward action. It was a crucial first step for him knowing how to use his imagination, optimism, and self-searching to uncover and discover himself.

While continuing to open up to his authentic self, he is leaving space for serendipity and discouraging a myopic path forward. When you turn toward exploring your own interests, do so with wonder. Neil Armstrong's famous words are

CONCLUSION

emblazoned on a plaque at Cape Canaveral: "Mystery creates wonder, and wonder is the basis for man's desire to understand." By exploring with a sense of wonder, you are on the right path to pursuing your calling.

You were born curious. As a result of institutionalized learning and social myths, your curiosity and sense of exploration has been slowly sapped away from your default mindset. But you know that there is something inherent in you that is limitless. You can push yourself into new experiences and accomplishments you never thought possible. Getting back in touch with your wondrous self can change your community and the world. As you turn the final pages of this book, it is now up to you to cultivate your own mindset of wonder. Doing so is part and parcel to your engine of curiosity and growth.

Starting today, begin again by pursuing your imagination. Jumpstart your sense of wonder toward your ambitions. Set goals. Adventurously explore your many paths on the way to accomplishing your dreams. The things you once thought impossible will become possible. What will happen if you open yourself up to serendipity? Things might work out. They might not. Or something unexpected will happen, taking you into a new adventure you hadn't conceived of. Draw yourself into being like Harold from *Harold and the Purple Crayon*. Wade through the frightening and terrifying newness of it all. By being a revised version of yourself, you will create a different life. Start scaffolding life on your own terms.

With *The Wonder Effect*, you give yourself permission to believe in yourself. Further, you will also believe in your potential. Believing in yourself, go exploring. While on your journey, look to break the mold. In a world of height, Spud Webb and Muggsy Bogues were short NBA players who became superstars. For them as for you, the standards did not restrict them. Adventurous exploration should be guided by new standards, failures, and lessons along the way, a growth mindset, and an openness that generates a joy for the journey.

ENJOY THE ADVENTURE

One of my favorite authors is Dr. Benjamin Hardy, as you may have surmised by this point. In his book *Personality Isn't Permanent*, Dr. Hardy argues that folks mistakenly shape their own limitations by arbitrarily bestowing them on themselves.* This echoes some of my earlier ideas. "I'm not a car guy," somebody might say. Of course, they won't be a "car guy" with an attitude like that! Who you are is your choice, and you also get to choose your purpose for living. Dr. Hardy explains, "Your purpose isn't something you discover, but something you ultimately choose yourself. Stop looking for it

---

* Benjamin Hardy, *Personality Isn't Permanent: Break Free from Self-Limiting Beliefs and Rewrite Your Story* (London: Portfolio, 2020).

CONCLUSION

and make the choice, then allow that choice to transform you."*

Whatever your behaviors are, you become that personality. Therefore, any given moment is your opportunity to create the personality you prefer. Dr. Hardy continues:

> Without a deep sense of purpose, your personality will be based on avoiding pain and pursuing pleasure, which is an animalistic and low-level mode of operating. This is the common view and approach to personality for most. However, when you're driven by purpose, you'll be highly flexible and you'll make decisions irrespective of pain and pleasure to create and become who you want.†

You are not locked into a particular personality. You may have certain faults or quirks, but even those can be changed if you so choose. If you are currently an uncreative person, there are ways to grow your creativity. If you want to be a numbers person, there are paths you can take. Practice being extraordinary with these interests to confirm your new identity. Get comfortable with being uncomfortable. When you attempt the extraordinary, you generate the experience necessary to gain real expertise.

---

* Hardy, *Personality Isn't Permanent*, 49.
† Hardy, *Personality Isn't Permanent*.

Take a leap of faith that you can be who you want to be.

When I was sixteen years old, I was vacationing at Elephant Butte Lake. My friends and I sat near the top of a small cliff overlooking the lake. It was around a hundred-feet drop. We agreed it would be a thrill to jump down into the pristine lake. But looking over the edge, we were terrified. My fear had me second-guessing. Author and podcast host James Altucher says that if he doesn't feel a sense of fear before publishing his writing, he knows the writing is probably no good. Sensing that fear, I knew I was engaged in an experience that might give me a new perspective or experience. Using my fear to stay composed and aware, I made my leap of faith. I splashed down and crossed an item off of my bucket list.

I'm not telling you to literally jump off of a cliff, but I am telling you to take a leap of faith and bet on yourself. You can develop the capacity to pursue those interests that will lead to an impactful and life-changing experience. Jump off the proverbial cliff and build your plane on the way down, purple crayon in hand.

Pull the threads of your interests to ignite your passions and pursue your calling. Create a wondrous life by wondering what is possible and being willing to explore that. Let that sustain your constant movement.

Go wonder!

ACKNOWLEDGMENTS

It says in the Talmud to express gratitude daily. Why? Because daily we face mortal danger, often unaware, and because those who experience a miracle often don't sense the miracle taking place. Completing this book was only possible because of a string of miracles for which I would like to give thanks.

I credit the Lubavitcher Rebbe for positively changing the trajectory of my life and the lives of millions of others. I will always be indebted to the enrichment of his influence and teachings.

My life has been formed and influenced in so many ways, whether from family, friends, teachers, mentors, bosses, or people even willing to help me a bit. Below, I've tried to simply recognize and acknowledge all those who in large and small ways have contributed to making me who I am today. It's extremely eclectic and may seem very disconnected. I've even

ACKNOWLEDGMENTS

included some childhood friends who, while I don't still have any contact with them, were those I spent time with, played with, got in trouble with, and, most importantly, used my imagination and creativity with. I'm also grateful to all those friends and neighbors who I spent time with, rejoiced with, laughed with, and traveled with. There are some mentors and influences that may have played seemingly minor roles but have most definitely impacted me in ways that have lasted. Family has always been important to me, and I'm grateful to my immediate family to whom I've dedicated this work, but also to those who preceded me and those who I may have spent very little time with likely due to the constraints of geography; nevertheless, that sense of familiarity when you are with them, perhaps because of their sense of humor or little nuances of expressions, is something that I treasure, that I'm lucky to have, and I would wish that everyone has a place either geographically or in their hearts they can call home.

FAMILY MEMBERS (SPOUSE, CHILDREN, PARENTS, SIBLINGS)

Esther, Mendel, Miriam, Devora Leah, Zalman, Yossi, Chaim Meir, and Shimmy

Dad, Mom and Joe

Caryn and Cory, thanks for giving me such an amazing wife and mother

ACKNOWLEDGMENTS

Jessica, Bluma, Sara

Bluma's kids, Jessica's kids

Shayna and Menachem and kids

Davi and Rachel and Bailey

Elie Azoff-Slifstein

Bill and Beverly Azoff

Ernie and Estelle Lumer

Uncle Arnie Alt and his family

Uncle Richy Alt and his family

Aunt Suzie Hogan and her family

Grandpa Sam and Grandma Estelle

Grandparents Charles and Rachel Haston

Howard and Elaine Alt and their family

Marla Alt and Jeff

FRIENDS

Sarah and Chaim Baruch Alevsky, R' Ari and Leah Sollish, Yoni Katz, Michoel Shapiro, R' Enan and Gitty Francis, Abi and Tzipora Vail, Yanky and Ahuva Borenstein, David and

ACKNOWLEDGMENTS

Rivka Kasle, R' Baruch and Raizy Kaplan, Motti and Miriam Sandman, Levi and Sarah Bartfield, Mendy and Dini Edelkopf, Judy and Stuart Levitz, Beth and Rolly Lopez, Sydney and Meralee Schlusselberg, Yair and Shira Moskowitz, Hank and Suzy Rothschild, David Azzerad, Zev and Leah Sandman, Zalman and Gittel Roth, Chezkel and Bailh Eidelman, Aryeh and Leah Caroline, Chezky and Chaya Hinda Holtzberg,, Mendy and Devorah Katz, Mendel and Kayla Gurevitch, Eli and Dini Katz, Schneur and Bluma Katz, Levi and Shaindy Brackman, Sholom and Rosie Andrusier, Yossi Levitin, Arileh Kanevsky, R' Eli and Rochelle Raskin, Yitz and Zisa Levine, Laibi Vail, Dan Scherban, David and Suri Waren, Yasef and Bassie Deitsch, Mendel and Basya Deitsch, R' Yosef Lustig, Nechemia and Gittel Chana Levine, Yona Fenton, Michael Linder, Chezky and Libby Herz, R' Yechiel Cagan, R' Mendy and Altie Kasowitz, R' Shmueli Novak, R' Levi Mendelow, R' Mendy Hecht, R' Schneur Wilhelm, R' Rami and Deb Strosberg, Mattis and Deb Sessel, Louis Berkowitz, Tracy Saxe, Aviv and Corrine Aviad, Ronny Modiano, Dr. Doug Duchen, Odded Benjamin, Dr. Ninivaggi, Jeff and Randy Marks, The Know-It-All Brothers, Sydney Perry, Yael Benoit, Charles and Melissa Rosenay, Jonathan and Irit Perkins, Rich and Shelly Gans, Roger and Judith Hess, Elicia and Joe Kusnitz, Alana Rosenberg, Litan Yahav, Calvin Chin, Josh McCallen, Jake Harris, Leigh Archer, Greg Kaplan, Michael Hanna, Glenn Hanson, R' Dovid Dick, Robert and Ida Dick, Charlie Kushner, Albie Rosenhaus, Johnny Pirkle,

ACKNOWLEDGMENTS

Adam Ambrose, Bernie May, Dana Rubin, Michael Herman, Bruce, Brother Christopher, Father Freddie, Sensei, Ronen Zekry, Lyndon Kan, Shaun Hurwitz, Gernot Bruckner, Fernando Pastor, Mark and Dahlia Nordlicht, Kevin Shacknofsky, Jeff Kiderman, Nathan and Julie Thomas, Shlomo Ressler, Dr. Judy Stoner.

EDITORS & PEOPLE WHO WORKED ON THE BOOK PRODUCTION

This simply wouldn't have happened without the help and guidance of Nicholas Potter, Tim McConnehey, and Jenna Love.

TEACHERS / MENTORS / BOSSES

R' Gafni, R' Bolton, R' Cohen, R' Greenberg, R' Strosberg, R' Shochet, R' Hecht, R' Kessler, R' Yaffe, R' Manis Friedman, Edward Teller, Marty Marshall, Mitch Albom, Dennis Prager, Michael Gerber, Jim Sheils.

INFLUENTIAL PEOPLE AND/OR PODCASTS IN MY OUTLOOK OR WAY OF THINKING

Tim Ferris, James Altucher, Stephen Dubner, Steven Levitt, Noah Kagan, Hal Elrod, Brian Keating, Reid Hoffman, Brendan Bruchard, A.J Jacobs, Adam Grant, Carol Dweck, Dan

ACKNOWLEDGMENTS

Sullivan, Ryan Holiday, Oren Klaff, Julia Cameron, Cameron Herold, Edith Eger, David Goggins, Malcolm Gladwell, Stephen Covey, Brené Brown, Stephen West, Jim Kwik, Sam Parr, Shaan Puri, Steven West, *GoBundance, Bigger Pockets, Into the Impossible, My First Million, Philosophize This, Masters of Scale, Freakonomics Radio.*

"This is a powerful guide to unlocking passion and purpose. It helps you reconnect with your natural curiosity and realize you're not bound by convention. With a fresh perspective on growth and possibility, this book empowers you to break free from limitations and create a life that truly excites you."

—Jason Wasser, LMFT, Host of
You Winning Life Podcast and Founder of
The Family Room Wellness Associates

"Having worked closely with Adam Haston in educational leadership, I'm continually inspired by his ability to challenge the status quo. *The Wonder Effect* captures his depth, curiosity, and bold thinking, pushing readers to see success differently. This book will challenge conventions, shift perspectives, and inspire transformative growth."

—Rabbi Rami Strosberg, Educator and Musician

"*The Wonder Effect* is a refreshing and thought-provoking read, weaving together life's lessons with deep insights and practical wisdom. With Adam's keen ability to ask the right questions and encourage meaningful reflection, this book offers a detailed framework that invites readers to explore life with curiosity, resilience and intention—essential qualities for personal growth and transformation."

—Bluma Sapir, PsyD, Psychologist and Author of
*I'm Right, You're Stupid: Growing Up
Your Sibling Relationship*

"*The Wonder Effect* is more than a guide—it's an invitation to live boldly, think fearlessly, and take control of your future.

"I've known Adam Haston for 17 years, and he doesn't just talk about chasing big ideas—he lives them. His curiosity is relentless, his generosity is real, and his passion for pushing boundaries is contagious. This book challenges you to step beyond comfort, embrace adventure, and create a life that excites you."

—Tracy Alan Saxe, President and CEO of *SDV Law Group*

"In a fast-paced world demanding adaptability, *The Wonder Effect* is your roadmap to a more fulfilling life. Adam Haston reveals the power of curiosity, resilience, and strategic thinking to navigate challenges and seize opportunities. Whether in business, leadership, or personal growth, this book inspires bold action and empowers you to embrace change, think bigger, and create your own success story."

—Andrew Johnson, Managing Director, *London | Green*

"*The Wonder Effect* is like water after months in the desert—refreshing, revitalizing, and transformative. Adam Haston masterfully weaves wisdom and actionable insights, reigniting curiosity and inspiring readers to break free from societal myths, challenge limitations, and embrace exploration. This book is a must-read for anyone seeking clarity, direction, and the courage to pursue their true calling."

—Uziel Vishedsky, Entrepreneur

"Climbing Kilimanjaro with Adam, I witnessed his unique way of thinking—challenging perspectives, inspiring curiosity, resilience, and purpose. *The Wonder Effect* encourages readers to rethink possibilities, embrace growth, and create meaningful impact. A compelling read for anyone ready to break boundaries and live with intention."

—Shmuel Gniwisch, Founder and Managing Partner, *Kli Capital*

"In *The Wonder Effect*, Adam Haston delivers an inspiring and practical roadmap for anyone looking to create a life of purpose and success. With clarity and heart, he shares hard-earned lessons and actionable strategies that help readers tap into their own potential. This book isn't just about personal growth—it's about redefining what's possible."

—Levi Brackman, PhD, Author of *Jewish Wisdom for Business Success*, Host of *Truths* Podcast, and CEO of *Invown*

"Adam's unique writing style makes fundamental principles easy to absorb and apply in real-life situations. *The Wonder Effect* challenges readers to rethink what they know and discover new perspectives for growth and success. No matter where you are on your journey, this book offers valuable insights to help you move forward with purpose."

—Rabbi Yoni Katz, Director, *Chabad of YouTube*

"From our first interaction at Harvard Business School, Adam Haston stood out for his love and light. The greatest distinction in personal growth is between those who know and those who truly live it—Adam is the latter. *The Wonder Effect* distills real-life lessons that challenge beliefs, inspire self-leadership, and guide you toward a life of purpose and service."

—Tony Nicholson, Entrepreneur, Best-Selling Author of *Core Health: 8 Simple Steps to Creating Balanced Life*, and Coach

"I've known Adam for years and continue to marvel at his boundless curiosity, infectious enthusiasm, and fearless pursuit of wisdom. He embraces the unknown, challenges assumptions, and explores new ideas with an open heart. *The Wonder Effect* is a reflection of his passion—an invitation to embrace wonder, take risks, and live with greater meaning and purpose."

—Rabbi Ari Sollish, Author of *Inclusion and the Power of the Individual*, and Director of *The Torah Center of Atlanta*

"*The Wonder Effect* was a revelation. It was an amalgam of many of my curiosities answered in a way that was succinct and artful. I left the reading more aware of my own mind's limitations and the limitations that I may have imposed on those closest to me."

—Web Smith, Commerce Executive, Consultant, Founder, *2PM Inc*, Distance Runner, Father, and Husband

ABOUT THE AUTHOR

Adam Haston, is an entrepreneur, educator, and leader dedicated to helping others unlock their potential. The founder and CEO of Haston Equity Group, a financial and real estate firm, he combines business acumen with a passion for personal growth. A former rabbi and director of programming at Chabad in Connecticut, Haston learned that transformation begins with truly listening. He has mentored professionals, students, and entrepreneurs, guiding them through career transitions, personal challenges, and leadership development. He has led workshops on financial success, personal growth, and resilience. His philanthropic work includes fundraising for schools, synagogues, and the Friendship Circle. A lifelong adventurer, Haston has climbed Mount Kilimanjaro, run the NYC Marathon, and traveled the world, but his greatest journey is as a devoted husband to Esther and father to seven incredible children. You can learn more at www.adamhaston.com

www.ingramcontent.com/pod-product-compliance
Lightning Source LLC
Chambersburg PA
CBHW030138170426
43199CB00008B/119